DON'T LET THE WORLD PASS YOU BY!

52 REASONS TO HAVE A PASSPORT

BY

SARA BENSON
COORDINATING AUTHOR

**CHRIS BATY, TOM DOWNS, JULIE GRUNDVIG,
THOMAS KOHNSTAMM, ROBERT REID,
REGIS ST LOUIS, RYAN VER BERKMOES,
CHINA WILLIAMS, KARLA ZIMMERMAN**

PREFACE BY **PHIL KEOGHAN**

INTRODUCTION BY **TONY WHEELER**

LONELY PLANET PUBLICATIONS

MELBOURNE • OAKLAND • LONDON

Don't Let the World Pass You By! 52 Reasons to Have a Passport
Published September 2005

Published by Lonely Planet Publications Pty Ltd

Head office:
90 Maribyrnong Street, Footscray, Vic 3011, Australia
Locked Bag 1, Footscray, Vic 3011, Australia

Branches:
150 Linden Street, Oakland CA 94607, USA
72-82 Rosebery Avenue, Clerkenwell, London EC1R 4RW, UK

ISBN 1 74059 578 5

text © Lonely Planet Publications Pty Ltd 2005

Cover Photographs:
Lonely Planet Images: Caraboa © Eric L Wheater; Corbis/APL: Elephant © Dallas & John Heaton,
Donkey © Bojan Breceli, Scooter © Larry Williams, Camel © Wolfgang Kaehler
Internal Photograph: p63 © Karla Zimmerman

Lonely Planet and the Lonely Planet logo
are trademarks of Lonely Planet Publications Pty. Ltd.
Printed by Quebecor World, Kingsport TN
Printed in USA

PREFACE

BY PHIL KEOGHAN,
host of Emmy Award-winning TV show *The Amazing Race*,
and author of *No Opportunity Wasted* (www.noopportunitywasted.com).

★ ★ ★

I HAD MY FIRST PASSPORT WHEN I WAS TWO YEARS OLD. (MY OWN DAUGHTER GOT HER FIRST PASSPORT WHEN SHE WAS TWO WEEKS OLD.) By the time I was 12, I had traveled extensively throughout the Americas. I even flew by myself from the Caribbean back to New Zealand to attend boarding school. I got the travel bug early. Now every time I look up and see a plane in the sky, I dream of somewhere new.

It's imperative that we get students curious and hungry about the world early. The most opportune time to travel is straight out of school, when you can just pack your bags and go. Travel is the most valuable education money can't buy – an opportunity to be resourceful and learn lessons that will affect the way we live the rest of our lives.

As people grow older, they become more rigid in their ways of thinking. They make up more excuses. They make the assumption that they can only leave their house and go overseas if they have a lot of time and money. My whole philosophy is that imagination is your currency, not the money you have in your wallet.

Americans often tell me, "But we've got it all here. We've got every culture." Americans do have a lot, but not everything. My favorite moments on *The Amazing Race* are when we have people from Texas, for example, who have never crossed the border, never owned passports, and never left their home state. When they end up in a place like India, it's as if they've landed on another planet. There's nowhere that you can go in America that's like Calcutta. This kind of experience gives you perspective, and a different understanding of the world.

Fear stops many of us from getting on planes. One of the things that excites me about *The Amazing Race* is that millions of viewers see everyday people in the Arab world, Asia and everywhere else doing acts of kindness for Americans. Those are powerful images. *The Amazing Race* allows you to vicariously experience the world, but I promise you it's even better in person.

I've found out that having a passport ultimately isn't so much about the places that it allows you to go as the people who want to share their world with you. When people travel, they do talk about the postcard images they've seen of say, Patagonia, but what they really remember is the human connections they make.

I've always had a passport. In a true sense, it's a ticket to your dreams. Travel is about immersing yourself in something new, allowing yourself to be a fish out of water and just trusting that things will work out. It may not be like home, but so what? It doesn't have to be. It's time to get lost. This book will show you how. The world is waiting for you!

INTRODUCTION

BY TONY WHEELER,
co-founder of Lonely Planet Publications

★ ★ ★

"THE WORLD IS A BOOK AND THOSE WHO DO NOT TRAVEL READ ONLY A PAGE," said St Augustine. I've spent most of my life trying to read as much as possible. I've always wondered if Mark Twain's excellent observation that **"there ain't no surer way to find out whether you like people or hate them than to travel with them"** applied to his travel companions or the people he traveled among, but traveling has taught me that I like nearly everybody.

Take Iran, a country not on everybody's "most friendly" list. I spent a couple of weeks there in 2004, and I can't remember the last time I was treated with such hospitality. The Iranians like to picnic, and every time I walked through a park I seemed to get invited over to join somebody's picnic. Perhaps it's because tourists are pretty unusual there, but an awful lot of Iranians want to talk to you, and a surprising number of them speak English and want to practice it. They also like to drink tea, and I never visited a tea house without a waiter or a fellow tea drinker coming over for a chat. While dining alone in restaurants, I'd regularly get invited over to join another table. By the end of my visit I had a collection of photographs with Iranian families who wanted me to join the family snapshot. "Well," I thought, "so this is what life is like on the Axis of Evil."

TONY'S TOP TEN TRAVEL SURPRISES

1. UNITED ARAB EMIRATES Iran, Iraq and Saudi Arabia may be close neighbors, but the UAE boasts Dubai, one of the most amazingly modern cities in the world; there you can get a cold beer in a bar and women can lounge on the beach in bikinis.

2. BOTSWANA With friendly people, good roads, great lodges and campsites, this is another country where you quickly discover that the myths are wrong and African travel is easy and amazingly rewarding.

3. BURMA (MYANMAR) An incompetent and unpleasant government doesn't mean that the people aren't wonderfully warm and welcoming; for them, you're an important contact with the outside world.

4. CHINA It's fascinating to visit a country where things are changing at warp speed. Despite their race to catch up with the first world, the Chinese have also become much more relaxed in recent years.

5. ITALY Spend any time in Italy and you'll soon realize that all those clichés about Italian style, fine food, great wine, fast cars, faster motorcycles and a passion for opera and soccer are absolutely true.

Or take France? Snooty, aloof and they make fun of your inability to speak their great language, right? Well, I lived in Paris for a year in the mid-'90s, and I started every morning with a jog around my neighborhood, concluding with stops at the newsstand to buy a paper and at the patisserie to buy bread (the best bread in the world, as long as you eat it within half an hour of buying it). After a week of that regular morning circuit I'd become a fixture, somebody to be greeted with a cheery *"bonjour, Monsieur"* and a quick French lesson. Aloof? Snooty? Forget about it!

Take rich and poor. Somehow we in the developed world, the first world, have gotten the idea that it takes money to be happy. Tell that to a group of islanders from the tiny Pacific nation of Tuvalu who party like there's no tomorrow. Go to a village dance on the magical Indonesian island of Bali, and you'll begin to wonder why anybody ever bothered to invent television. Take a trek in Nepal, and it's clearly obvious how proud your Sherpa camping crew is of the beautiful Himalayas and the excellent job they do in guiding you along the mountain trails.

Take religion. Of course, it's interesting to come into contact with other people's religions, whether it's Buddhism in Thailand, Hinduism in India or Islam in any of the Arab countries, but it can be a real surprise to run into some of the earliest reminders of Christianity in Syria. "Didn't you realize this was one of the places where Christianity started?" your Syrian hosts may explain. Or go to Ethiopia, where monks painstakingly produced illuminated manuscripts centuries before a quill pen was ever dipped in ink in a European monastery.

Travel is full of pleasant surprises, but it's also enormously important for many other reasons, ranging from economics to global relations. International trade and business become more important every day, and you won't even comprehend the market, let alone make the sale, if you don't know the marketplace. It's through travel, first and foremost, that we meet and understand the outside world. We can read all about other countries in papers and magazines or see them on television, but it's remarkable how different places turn out to be when you actually visit them. The media feed us scare stories about those in other countries, but the reality is that most people in the world are searching for the same things we are – a better life, a better future for their children – and they're only too ready to lend a hand to a fellow human being. Today, traveling to other countries is more important than it has ever been.

TONY'S TOP TEN TRAVEL SURPRISES

6. THAILAND It really is the "Land of Smiles." The Thais are as confident as the French; they simply know they have the best food and the strongest culture in Asia.

7. ARGENTINA While you're wandering the streets of Buenos Aires, catch an impromptu tango performance in some picturesque square, and you'll soon be signing up for lessons.

8. SYRIA Another country where reputation and reality are two different things. Roman ruins, ancient Christian sites and Crusader castles mix with Arab mosques and a passion for vintage American autos.

9. BHUTAN In this tiny patch of mountain magic, the national sport is archery and the government's official aim is to improve Gross National Happiness.

10. PAPUA NEW GUINEA It's been dubbed a "parliament of a thousand tribes," and the mighty Sepik River is a living art gallery.

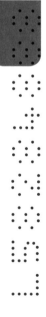

The Authors

SARA BENSON / COORDINATING AUTHOR

PLACE OF BIRTH: **ILLINOIS**

FIRST PASSPORT STAMP:
NARITA AIRPORT, TOKYO, JAPAN

REASONS #: **1, 17, 37, 51**

Back in the '80s, naive Midwestern kids who had never crossed the Mississippi before were airlifted over the Pacific for summer exchange programs in **Japan,** courtesy of the Mazda corporation. After her mom drove her down to the passport agency in Chicago, Sara soon found herself speeding on a bullet train to **Hiroshima.** When she was 18, she spent another summer working in **London,** then hitchhiked for a month around **Ireland,** where her family is from. Addicted to travel, the next year she rode slow (ie, cheap) trains all the way from **Paris** to **Sicily,** where she just missed the boat to **Tunisia.** Later, after graduating from college with a futile liberal arts degree, she taught English in **Kyūshū** and wandered for a few years through the wilds of **Asia,** racking up thousands of miles on broken-down Chinese trains, rickety **Laos** buses and all sorts of roads on foot. Today, when she's not lost in the tangled alleyways of **Moroccan** medinas, climbing volcanoes in the Pacific Rim or relic hunting on Route 66, she's at home in **California.**

CHRIS BATY

PLACE OF BIRTH: **CALIFORNIA**

FIRST PASSPORT STAMP:
CHARLES DE GAULLE AIRPORT, PARIS, FRANCE

REASONS #: **13**

Chris Baty picked up his first passport at the tender age of 15, to attend a study abroad summer program in **France.** Immediately impressed by a land where teenagers were allowed to drink alcohol, he resolved to spend more time investigating the world's other intoxicating cultural differences. Somewhere along the way, he's gone through two more passports and managed to visit most of continental **Western Europe,** as well as **Hungary, Greece, the Czech Republic** and **Singapore.** Despite the many wonders he's encountered, his favorite destination is the one that put the first mark on his passport's virgin pages.

★ **8** ★

TOM DOWNS

PLACE OF BIRTH: **CALIFORNIA**

FIRST PASSPORT STAMP:
ORLY AIRPORT, PARIS, FRANCE

REASONS #: **18, 22, 41**

Tom's world travels got a kick start when, at age 20, he won a free flight from Los Angeles to **Paris.** Needless to say, he rushed out and got his passport. He also grabbed a Eurail pass and spent the summer railroading around **Western Europe.** He saw bullfights in **Spain,** hiked partway up the Matterhorn and slept under the bridges of **Paris.** Since then, Tom has journeyed to Europe several times, and he's been to **Australia** and **Southeast Asia** on many occasions. Travel abroad has also inspired him to explore the USA more thoroughly, and he now makes a living as a travel writer. Tom lives in Oakland, **California,** with his wife, Fawn, and their children, Mai, Lana and Liam.

JULIE GRUNDVIG

PLACE OF BIRTH: **UTAH**

FIRST PASSPORT STAMP:
CHIANG KAI-SHEK AIRPORT, TAIWAN

REASONS #: **21, 24, 26, 38**

Julie received her first US passport when she traveled to **Taiwan** in the early 1990s. Over the past 14 years, she has traveled extensively throughout **north** and **Southeast Asia, Central Asia** and **Europe.** Currently associate editor for the international journal *Yishu: Journal of Contemporary Chinese Art,* she now lives in **Vancouver, Canada.**

THOMAS KOHNSTAMM

PLACE OF BIRTH: WASHINGTON STATE

FIRST PASSPORT STAMP:
GATWICK AIRPORT, LONDON, UNITED KINGDOM

REASONS #: 3, 7, 8, 19, 20, 23, 27, 28, 32, 39

Thomas owes his interest in international travel to his parents, Linda and Ed, who journeyed around the world in the late '60s. They hauled Thomas and his brother James all over **Europe** and **Northern Africa,** taking in the Rock of Gibraltar and Stonehenge, **Spanish** bullfighting and (relatively more dangerous) **Yugoslavian** soccer, and delicious **Italian** food and not-so-delicious **English** food, among other things. At 17, Thomas first traveled by himself, working as a translator at an international culture festival in northern Spain. Before he had finished high school, he was back visiting new friends in **Munich** and **Amsterdam.** After another stint in Spain, he headed to **Argentina** as a university exchange student in the mid-'90s. He visited practically every country in the region, learned **Portuguese,** worked in **Ecuador** and **Costa Rica** and lived in **Rio.** Thomas returns to **Latin America** and the **Caribbean** whenever possible and has also traveled with his brother in **India** and a tiny bit of **Nepal.** When not on the road, he can be found in his hometown of **Seattle.**

ROBERT REID

PLACE OF BIRTH: VIRGINIA

FIRST PASSPORT STAMP:
GATWICK AIRPORT, LONDON, UNITED KINGDOM

REASONS #: 4, 16, 35, 42, 50

Raised in Oklahoma, a wide-eyed Robert posed for his first passport photo at age 20, before leaving on a **London**-to-**Rome** blitz with a Eurail pass and a much-overpacked backpack. The travel bug had bitten little Robert long before – somewhere between vomiting in a new sombrero in **Puerto Vallarta** at age 8 and getting bitten by a gerbil on Canada Day (en route to **Banff**) at age 9. Since then, he's handed his passport to immigration folk in over 30 countries (and lost one once in **Guadalajara**). He's lived in **Russia, Vietnam, Australia** and **London,** and traveled throughout **Southeast Asia, Europe** and **Central America.** When not in **Plovdiv, San Cristóbal de las Casas, Mrauk U** or **Komsomolsk,** he's at home in **Brooklyn,** where he writes, eats fig bars and bores willing ears with tales of being followed by an ex-KGB agent in **Moscow,** contending with **Saigon** rats, giving an interview to a **Bulgarian** newscaster with purple hair, and being captivated by the size of a camel's nostril in **India.**

REGIS ST LOUIS

PLACE OF BIRTH: **INDIANA**

FIRST PASSPORT STAMP:
ZAGREB AIRPORT, YUGOSLAVIA (NOW CROATIA)

REASONS #: **30, 31, 33, 34, 36, 40, 47, 52**

Regis was 16 when his parents invited him on a religious pilgrimage to southwestern **Yugoslavia.** Although it wasn't his first-choice destination, the trip into the unknown made a deep impression on him. The strolls through idyllic villages, early-morning ascents up holy mountains and nightly brandy-tasting sessions filled him with wanderlust, and he decided to spend the rest of his life learning languages and traveling the world – once he got his driver's license. After high school Regis traveled north to Indiana University, where he studied Slavic languages and literature, and then spent a long year in **Russia** and **Ukraine.** Regis' focus soon shifted to tropical countries. Following a momentous trip to **Peru** in the late '90s, he sold all of his belongings and set out on a trip across **Latin America.** Although he ran out of money in **Panama,** the trip proved fortuitous, as it led to a career in travel writing. He lives in **New York City.**

RYAN VER BERKMOES

PLACE OF BIRTH: **CALIFORNIA**

FIRST PASSPORT STAMP:
GATWICK AIRPORT, LONDON, UNITED KINGDOM

REASONS #: **44, 46, 48**

Ryan got his first passport on July 30, 1984, in order to go backpacking in **Europe.** He quit his job as an investigative reporter in Chicago and boarded a People Express 747 bound for **London.** Somehow managing to be both bleary-eyed and wide-eyed at the same time, he boarded a train to Victoria Station. In an effort to avoid the pasty-faced glares of the morning commuters (the lot of them irritated at yet another backpacker crowding their space), Ryan looked out the window to see his first sight of the English countryside: a McDonald's Big Mac box lying along the tracks. Fortunately, things soon got more interesting. Since then, Ryan's travels have taken him worldwide, from **Afghanistan** to the **Arctic Sea, Brazil** to **Bali, New Zealand** to **Northern Ireland, Singapore** to **Sri Lanka.** In his long career as a passport holder, his longest period between stamps was a mere four months. He also still sees McDonald's trash virtually everywhere but can recommend their toilets as a place of sanitary refuge – especially in **Russia.**

CHINA WILLIAMS

PLACE OF BIRTH: **CALIFORNIA**

FIRST PASSPORT STAMP:
FRANKFURT AIRPORT, GERMANY

REASONS #: **5, 6, 10, 49**

China first got her passport in high school for a summer exchange program in **Germany.** Her mother made her have the passport photo taken twice, rejecting the first one because she said it looked like China was on drugs (it was pollen season in South Carolina – honest). That same passport chaperoned her through a college tour of **Europe,** back when unsmiling border officials boarded the trains. But her second passport was the most sacred, bearing her favorite stamp: a page-long **Thai** visa that she got before moving abroad to teach English. Bold and inky, the stamp felt like a royal invitation to the exotic East. Stamps from **Vietnam, Cambodia** and **Laos** play minor roles in a passport otherwise dominated by numerous pilgrimages to **Thailand.** On the inaugural trip with her most recent passport, a US customs agent looked at China and then said, "Nice picture." She thinks it was a compliment. China, her passport and her husband live in **San Francisco.**

KARLA ZIMMERMAN

PLACE OF BIRTH: **OHIO**

FIRST PASSPORT STAMP:
BARAJAS AIRPORT, MADRID, SPAIN

REASONS #: **2, 9, 11, 12, 14, 15, 25, 29, 43, 45**

Karla acquired her first passport for a whirlwind Eurail tour that started in **Madrid** and ended in **Athens** nine countries later. Her photo at the time featured a spectacular mass of permed hair, a look that humbled her for the next 10 years. When she's not chained to her desk, Karla is a rabid traveler who might be found anywhere from the misty heights of **Machu Picchu** to the dripping jungles of **Angkor Wat** to the cumin-colored dunes of the **Sahara** to that tasty donut shop down the road. She has written travel features for books, newspapers, magazines and radio. She lives in **Chicago** with her partner, Eric, the ultimate trekking companion, who never says no and pays for it by having to endure everything from bus crashes in the **Vietnamese** highlands to Civil War reenactments in **Illinois.**

CONTENTS

⊕ **PASSPORTS:** A Short History of Your Ticket to the World
>>>>>>>>> **PAGE 14**

⊕ **IT'S EASY!** Five Steps to Get Your Passport
>>>>>>>>> **PAGE 18**

⊕ **ALL SYSTEMS GO!**
>>>>>>>>> **PAGE 21**

⊕ **IT'S ALL ABOUT YOU**
>>>>>>>>> **PAGE 51**

⊕ **EXPERIENCE IT FOR YOURSELF**
>>>>>>>>> **PAGE 78**

⊕ **CHANGE YOUR PERSPECTIVE**
>>>>>>>>> **PAGE 145**

⊕ **TOMORROW STARTS TODAY**
>>>>>>>>> **PAGE 163**

APPENDIX >>>>>>>>> **PAGE 179**
BEHIND THE SCENES >>>>>>>>> **PAGE 183**

PASSPORTS

A Short History of Your
Ticket to the World
by Sara Benson

★ ★ ★

IF YOU ALREADY HAVE A PASSPORT, YOU'RE IN THE MINORITY, HISTORICALLY SPEAKING. For most of recorded history, passports as we recognize them today haven't even existed. Where did they come from? When did they start being used? And why would you ever need one? The rest of this book answers the question "why," so let's attack "where" and "when."

Historians trace the first version of a passport to 450 BC, when Nehemiah, a Babylonian by birth, was appointed governor of Palestine. He didn't want to cross into unfamiliar territory without some sort of guarantee of safe passage, so the king of Persia drew up the paperwork. With this early passport in hand, Nehemiah made his way unscathed to Jerusalem.

In the ancient world travel was tough. Wars were common, and enemies were everywhere. There was nothing to protect you as you traveled – unless you happened to serve the Emperor of Rome, in which case a letter stating your citizenship would let you pass unharmed everywhere from Britain to Mesopotamia. That early Roman equivalent of a passport, the safe-conduct letter, might even entitle you to fresh vehicles and horses along the way. (Of course, some people who were granted safe conduct to Rome ended up being assassinated once they got there. But let's move on with our story, shall we?)

Throughout antiquity and the Middle Ages, only the privileged few (and some merchants) could travel. Most people were born, lived and died

★ "Passports and visas are the principal international frontier-

★ crossing documents.... The freedom to travel is a unique

★ instrument of friendly, peaceful communications among the

nations and the peoples of the world.... Direct personal

relationship enriches the lives of both the traveler and the

host, each borrowing from the other in customs, manners

and philosophy of life."

– 85TH US CONGRESS, second session (1958)

in the same village. Journeying abroad was unthinkable, unfeasible and, in some cases, illegal. The right to exit and enter your own country (except during times of war) wasn't written into law until King John imposed the Magna Carta in 1215. But even after that so few people traveled that, for a while, the Pope alone issued all of the safe-conduct letters in the Christian world (or so it's said).

The word "passport" first appeared in writing in mid-16th-century England. It evolved from the French words *passer* (to enter) and *port* (port or harbor). Keep in mind that, at that time, passports were required not only to travel abroad, but also to move about within the borders of one's own country, so the term might have also evolved from the word *porte*, referring to a town gate. Even if they were called by the same name as they are today, though, those early passports were nothing like the little booklets we carry now. Instead, they were elaborately handwritten, signed and sealed official letters valid for only one journey.

As Europe raced to establish colonies around the world, travel increased – and so did governmental controls of travelers. During the early days of British colonies in America, anyone who wished to travel abroad had to post notice of his intent to travel on a church door for two successive Sundays and to clear all of his debts. Only then could he apply to the governor, after which the courts had to approve his application for a passport.

With restrictions like that, it was easier to just stay home. Which, of course, was the point: passports were a way to prevent people from traveling, not to assist them. The American Revolution turned travel around. Citizens of the new United States of America suddenly were free to journey abroad (or to any other state) for the first time. Passports were issued by federal bureaucrats, state politicians, even city mayors. Diplomats abroad, including Benjamin Franklin in Paris, happily handed them out. Even foreigners could apply for US passports. In 1793 President George Washington issued one to a French balloonist named Jean Pierre Blanchard. The Frenchman only flew from Philadelphia to New Jersey (about 15 miles), but upon seeing Washington's signature on Blanchard's passport, the crowd was so impressed that they helped him back to Philly.

BY THE BOOK	TOTAL DIGITS IN A REGULAR US PASSPORT NUMBER:	PAGES IN A STANDARD US PASSPORT:	US PASSPORTS ISSUED BETWEEN 1801 AND 1809:	US PASSPORTS ISSUED IN 2004:	NUMBER OF PASSPORTS LAID END-TO-END REQUIRED TO STRETCH AROUND THE EQUATOR:
	NINE	24	FEWER THAN 600	8.8 MILLION	APPROXIMATELY 330 MILLION

In the early days of this country, all of the different US passports in circulation caused confusion. In 1856 the Department of State took control of issuing all passports, and US citizenship was required. Travel abroad exploded in the Victorian era, leading to the collapse of an overwhelmed passport system in Europe, while here at home the Civil War made having a passport essential; the documentation was necessary just to cross Union Army lines. Furthermore, you had to swear an oath of allegiance in order to get one. Demand was so high that the secretary of state was no longer able to personally sign each passport, so a stamp was used instead.

Enter the 20th century, with its world wars and advancing technology. Passports began to change rapidly, partly because more people could travel than ever before, but also because wars made travel control necessary. Passports became valid for a fixed time, instead of just one journey. Photographs were affixed to the folded sheet of paper that then constituted a passport.

For the first time, Uncle Sam charged a fee for issuing one. Passports also had to become sturdy and convenient to carry. A cloth cover was added (first a soft beige, then a hard green, and finally a hard red cover were tried). The folded piece of paper turned into a booklet that was scaled down to pocket size. Finally, passports needed to be more secure, and measures were taken to combat forgery and prevent counterfeiting. In 1952 the federal government made it official: henceforth, a passport would always be required of US citizens to exit or enter the country, not only during wartime. The cover changed to blue just before America's bicentennial in 1976.

Even today, the passport continues to evolve. But some things never change. Just like in ancient days, a passport tells the world who you are and where you're from, and helps make your passage around the globe safer. With it, you have the world in your pocket.

IT'S EASY!

Five Steps
to Get Your Passport
by Sara Benson

★ ★ ★

US governmental regulations and procedures can change at any time. By 2008 passports will be required for US citizens returning from all foreign countries by any means of transport, including Canada, Mexico and the Caribbean. Click to the US Department of State's Consular Affairs website (www.travel.state.gov/passport) for the latest information. Customer service representatives at the National Passport Information Center (NPIC; ☎ 877-487-2778, TDD/TTY 888-874-7793; ☾ 8am-8pm ET Mon-Fri, except federal holidays) can answer all of your questions; automated recorded information is available around the clock.

1. DO THE PAPERWORK

You'll need to fill out an application form to get your passport. All forms are available at any passport agency or acceptance facility (see Step 4) or you can download them off the Consular Affairs website.

2. SAY CHEESE!

With your passport application, you must submit two recent, identical, professional color photos (each measuring 2 inches by 2 inches) showing a full frontal view of your face against a plain white or off-white background. Wear normal street attire (no uniforms allowed). If you usually wear eyeglasses, do so in your passport photo. Dark glasses, hats and head coverings are not allowed, except for religious or medical purposes. Remember to smile!

Fast, affordable passport photos are available at FedEx Kinko (www.fedex kinkos.com), Walgreens (www.walgreens.com) and CVS (www.cvs.com).

3. GET OUT YOUR CHECKBOOK
Currently the application fee is $55 ($40 for minors under age 16), plus a $12 security fee. An execution fee of $30 is paid to the facility where you are applying. For an adult passport valid for 10 years, you'll pay $97 total. A passport issued to a minor aged 15 or younger costs $82 total and is only valid for five years. All fees are nonrefundable.

4. APPLY IN PERSON
Passport applications are accepted at more than 6000 facilities across the country, including some post offices. Check the Consular Affairs website or call the NPIC to find the location closest to you. If you are traveling within 14 days, or need your passport earlier for foreign visas, make an appointment to visit the nearest passport agency (currently these are found in Boston, MA; Chicago, IL; Honolulu, HI; Houston, TX; Los Angeles, CA; Miami, FL; New Orleans, LA; New York, NY; Norwalk, CT; Philadelphia, PA; San Francisco, CA; Seattle, WA; and Washington, DC); proof of travel is required.

> **PASSPORT 911**
>
> To protect yourself against identity theft, report a lost or stolen passport immediately to the State Department's Consular Lost/Stolen Passport Section (☎ 202-955-0430; ⏰9am-4pm EST Mon-Fri, except federal holidays). Your old passport number will be invalidated. A statement verifying that your passport was lost or stolen will be required for you to get a new passport. If you're abroad contact the nearest US embassy or consulate – your new passport can be expedited in five days. If you report your passport lost or stolen and then find it, do not use it for travel.

Be sure to bring your completed application, passport photos, an acceptable form of payment, your Social Security number, proof of citizenship (eg, birth certificate, certificate of naturalization or citizenship) and proof of identity (eg, current valid driver's license or government or military ID). Note that a Social Security card alone is not considered proof of identity. Minors under age 14 must appear in person with at least one parent or legal guardian and official written consent from the second parent or legal guardian. Additional documentation will be required to prove the identity of both parents or legal guardians, as well as their relationship to the child.

5. HURRY UP AND WAIT It takes about six weeks for routine processing of your passport application once it arrives at the passport agency. Expedited service, which costs $60 extra, takes about two weeks.

To check the status of your application, call the NPIC or visit www.travel.state.gov. When you receive your passport check that all the details are correct and call the NPIC if they are not. If the information is wrong the passport is invalid.

UH-OH, MY PASSPORT EXPIRED

If you were at least 16 years old when issued your last passport, it was issued less than 15 years ago and you still have the undamaged passport, you can renew your passport by mail for $67. Processing times are the same as if you apply in person. (If your legal name has changed, you must send a certified or notarized marriage certificate or court order with your application.) If you plan to travel a lot, you can request a larger 48-page passport at no extra cost (just include a signed letter of request with your application). If you reside abroad, and need to travel urgently, the embassy or consulate will issue you a temporary, limited-validity passport that you will have to turn in when you arrive at your destination, so that it can be replaced with a full-validity passport (at no extra charge). Remember, most other countries require that your passport be valid for six months beyond your dates of travel.

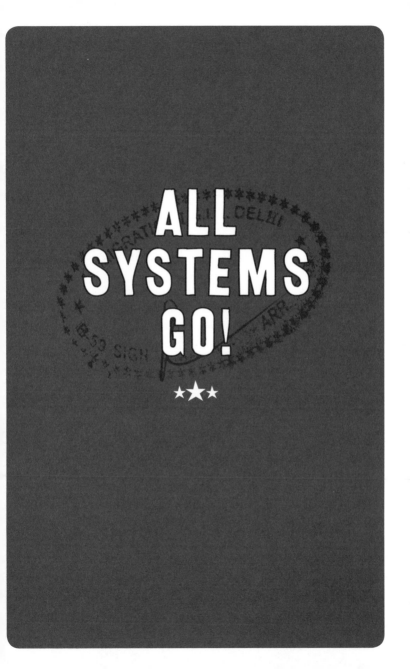

IT'S WHO YOU ARE

A PASSPORT IS YOUR TICKET TO DISTANT LANDS. But let's start closer to home. You might even be wondering: What exactly is a passport? And what's it got to do with me anyway?

A passport is the gold standard of personal identity. That small blue booklet with a flexible cover of woven cotton boasts state-of-the-art security measures, including digitized photo technology, secret designs that can be seen only under ultraviolet light, and soon a radio-frequency identification (RFID) chip to store the personal data found on the identification page and an electronic replica of your face. Thinking of forging a passport? Fuhgeddaboudit. If you pry the plastic off the identification page, you'll do serious damage; your now-invalid passport will declare loudly to any official who inspects it that it has been illegally tampered with.

Your passport can tell anyone who flips it open exactly who you are. In it your name, gender and date and place of birth are securely printed in machine-readable type. The probability of a doppelgänger being born in exactly the same place on the same date with the same name is unimaginably tiny. Your passport is almost as unique as your fingerprint. In fact, it's a federal crime for anyone else to use it.

In everyday life, a passport trumps all other government-issued

Surname:	
Given names:	
Nationality:	
Sex:	
Date of Birth:	Place of Birth:

ID cards. More inviolable than a driver's license and far more secure than your Social Security card, it packs a wallop worthy of Popeye in the halls of government bureaucracy. Any task that involves proving your identity – eg, replacing a lost driver's license, filling out tax forms, applying for a job – is simpler if you already have a passport in hand.

A passport is also your first step beyond ordinary life. Although your passport has your nationality stamped on the front cover, it's also your entry ticket into other nations. For many jet-set adventures, all you'll need is that little blue book. (Of course, to cross some international borders, you'll need to get a visa, too – see p47.)

The whole world is out there waiting for you. Don't let it pass you by! Just get your passport and go.

★ 23 ★

TAKING THAT FIRST STEP

The act of applying for a passport was actually my first international travel experience. I was excited and nervous, standing in line surrounded by people from around the world, talking in foreign tongues as I applied for this important document. To me, a passport was something almost mythic that movie characters whipped out with *savoir faire*. It was the all-important document that Allied POWs forged in the German camp scenes in *The Great Escape*. It was just as important to James Bond as any of his myriad gadgets. And when the United States of America issued me a passport two years before the state of New York would issue me a full-fledged driver's license – without making me take any tests – the world opened up to me. I felt closer to the places I had dreamed of traveling. And I no longer wondered *if* I would ever travel the globe, but only *when*.

— **ETHAN S**, SAN FRANCISCO

"PASSPORT, *n.* A document treacherously inflicted upon a citizen going abroad, exposing him as an alien and pointing him out for special reprobation and outrage."

- *The Devil's Dictionary* **BY AMBROSE BIERCE**, BORN IN OHIO IN 1842

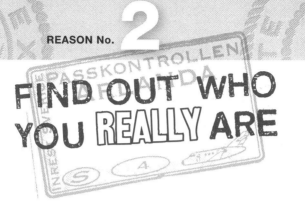

FIND OUT WHO YOU REALLY ARE

BILL CLINTON SCRAWLED HIS WAY THROUGH 1008 PAGES TO TELL HIS STORY IN THE MEMOIR *MY LIFE.* He could have saved a few trees by just publishing his passport.

A passport is an abridged version of one's history, or at least a 10-year chapter of it. To see how it works, open up the book and look at the inside cover, where you'll see a photo. Sporting a cutesy bob hair-cut? That's when you worked at a Fortune 500 company and hated it. A sneering guy with a ponytail stares out? Flashback to when you played bass in a punk band and loved it. As with all good plots, these characters are destined to change.

Flip to page 8 – a stamp from Manila, the Philippines. Ah, yes, the time when you jumped in a jeepney festooned with signboards declaiming a love for Jesus and got lost in the noisy streets of that crazy city. Turn to page 14 – an Auckland, New Zealand mark. That's where you bungee-jumped off a bridge, overcoming your fear of heights. Pages 3, 5, 15 and 16 show Rome imprints, attesting that you and an Italian boyfriend carried on a sexy, if impractical, bi-continental romance.

A passport can reveal a country's tale, too. Compare a bureaucratic-

BUT CAN A PASSPORT HELP ME FIT INTO MY FAVORITE PAIR OF JEANS? >>> REASON No. **15** looking Latvian visa from 1994 to a tiny, simple stamp for entering the country in 2003. It's clear a change has happened: Latvia has become less Soviet and more European. And a government overthrow turned a stamp from Zaire in 1996 into a stamp from the Democratic Republic of the Congo today.

Would you know these things about yourself – or the world – without a passport? **This official booklet not only makes your grand adventures possible, but also preserves them like photos in an album.** The epic story of how you got from here (the "place of birth" listed on the inside cover) to there (everywhere listed thereafter) is colored in shades of blue, green, red and purple ink. And should your story grow outsized, à la President Clinton, don't fret: simply apply for extra pages to be added to your passport (use Form DS-19), and keep on going.

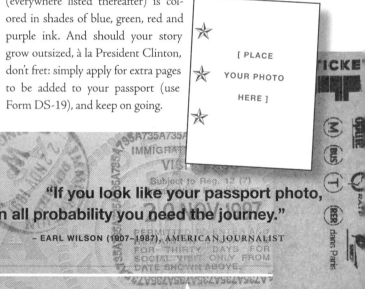

[PLACE YOUR PHOTO HERE]

"If you look like your passport photo, in all probability you need the journey."

– EARL WILSON (1907–1987), AMERICAN JOURNALIST

★★★
26

TOP 10 IRREVERENT, BUT NOT ILLEGAL, USES FOR YOUR PASSPORT >>>

1. Fan yourself seductively at an open-air café.

2. Beat off Italian men who want to pinch your ass.

3. Deflect snap-pops tossed by mischievous children during Chinese New Year.

4. Flush a foreign toilet without touching it directly.

5. Jimmy open the locked door to your hotel room.

6. Scratch the tropical bug bites on your back.

7. Fire up smoke signals if you get stranded on a deserted tropical island.

8. Create a flip animation book if bored while waiting for a bus or train.

9. Play "spin the passport" (fasten small paper arrow and spin for hours of fun).

10. Flash at bar bouncers back home when you lose your driver's license.

IIIIIIIIIIII I WANT TO DISCOVER MY INNER VAN GOGH. >>> REASON No. 35 IIIIIIIIIIIIIIIIIIIIII

EXERCISE YOUR RIGHTS

REMEMBER THE LAND OF THE FREE AND THE HOME OF THE BRAVE? Well, apparently we are still free, but not so many of us are feeling all that brave these days.

In the tradition of Teddy Roosevelt, Ernest Hemingway and Amelia Earhart, the doors are wide open for us as Americans to travel abroad and experience new things. Yet fewer than one in four Americans have their passport. In fact, that's the lowest percentage of passport-holding citizens of any nation in the developed world.

From Cuba to North Korea, citizens of many other nations are not allowed to leave their borders except in government-approved circumstances, if at all. In some African and Middle Eastern countries, a woman can't even apply for a passport without her husband's permission. Sounds like a travesty, no?

Having the opportunity to expand your life's experience beyond the US and not doing so is somewhat akin to having the right to vote and blowing off Election Day. Left unused, our freedoms can become just lofty words with little substance.

Beyond the personal benefits of international travel (more later), it's good for our country as a whole if you step outside our national borders. We live in an increasingly global world, and it's important for more Americans to understand the planet around us (no, watching FOX News or CNN doesn't count). A more complete grasp of the world, and of those living in it, will help us all progress in everything from business to politics to science to the arts.

Dare we say, it's patriotic to get your passport and travel abroad.

⋆ **What Our Founding Fathers Forgot** ⋆

Prior to independence, domestic and international travel were both heavily restricted in the American colonies. After 1776, however, passports were handed out like candy to jubilant US citizens, who were now free to travel as they liked – at least until wars later intervened. The new right to travel was taken for granted and never written into law. In truth, the US Constitution does not use the word "travel" even once, let alone establish an explicit right to travel. The right, however, is recognized in numerous court rulings throughout US history. In *Kent v Dulles*, Justice Douglas noted, "The right to travel is a part of the 'liberty' of which the citizen cannot be deprived without due process of law under the Fifth Amendment.... Freedom of movement across frontiers in either direction [is] a part of our heritage. Travel abroad...may be as close to the heart of the individual as the choice of what he eats, or wears, or reads. Freedom of movement is basic in our scheme of values."

⋆ 29 ⋆

BE AN AMBASSADOR

ARE YOU LOUD, INSENSITIVE AND DISMISSIVE OF ANYTHING THAT DOESN'T COME FROM THE BLOCK YOU GREW UP ON? Of course not. But some citizens of the world lump us all into that "ugly American" category, based on the actions of those travelers who are out of their element and outright misbehaving.

Some of the blame for bad behavior belongs in the "innocence of a child" column. A first exposure to The Other can set some travelers on their heels for a moment. Some of it also comes from forgetting where you are. Travelers who wouldn't dare comment on an iffy pasta sauce a friend brought to your Super Bowl party will loudly label pizza in Napoli as "rightly sucking" so that everyone overhears!

Let's change that perception. Carrying a passport abroad immediately makes you a spokesperson for us all. One of the thrills of traveling is making connections with people, and near the top of the list is hearing, "You're the first American I've met that's nice." It'll happen if you show saintly patience during the inevitable bumps in the road – a hotel that cannot change dollars, a foodstuff like you've never imagined or a warm cup of Coke.

Some worldly-wise travelers with a US passport are embarrassed by their fellow Americans on the road. Some apologize for them.

Others say they're from Canada (or even stick a maple leaf on their backpack). **Actually, it's much better to be yourself: be a pretty, not an ugly, American.** Remember that people are more willing to help if you can ask if they speak English in their language first.

But it doesn't stop there. The role of goodwill ambassador continues back home, where you can show off your newfound citizenship of the world (though there's no guarantee your friends and family will sit through your fourth soliloquy about riding horseback through Mongolia). In your town, watch out for visitors who need help using a phone or directions to the Arch. Once you've been lost and disoriented in another country, you'll know how right a day goes when a local smiles and says, "Where are you from?"

> **❝** People I met traveling abroad turned out to be kinder and more generous than I could have imagined. It's made me a nicer New Yorker. I actually stop and ask tourists if they need help now! **❞** – ADA C, NEW YORK

IIIIIIIIIIIIII **I'M MORE DIPLOMATIC WITH FELINES THAN MY OWN KIND.** IIIIIIIIIIIIIIIIIIIII
>>> REASON No. 37

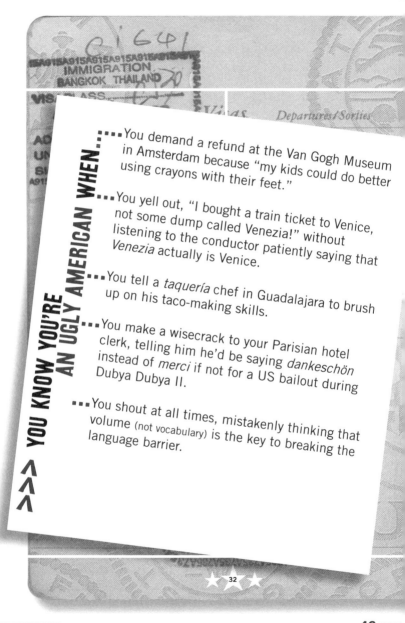

YOU KNOW YOU'RE AN UGLY AMERICAN WHEN...

···· You demand a refund at the Van Gogh Museum in Amsterdam because "my kids could do better using crayons with their feet."

···· You yell out, "I bought a train ticket to Venice, not some dump called Venezia!" without listening to the conductor patiently saying that *Venezia* actually is Venice.

···· You tell a *taquería* chef in Guadalajara to brush up on his taco-making skills.

···· You make a wisecrack to your Parisian hotel clerk, telling him he'd be saying *dankeschön* instead of *merci* if not for a US bailout during Dubya Dubya II.

···· You shout at all times, mistakenly thinking that volume (not vocabulary) is the key to breaking the language barrier.

> > >

★★ 32 ★★

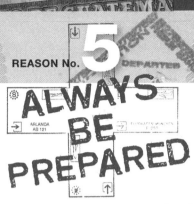

REASON No. 5

ALWAYS BE PREPARED

SO, YOU'RE A "JUST IN CASE" PERSON. **Look, you've got a stash of emergency cash, just in case. An umbrella in your car's trunk, just in case.** And you always buy the insurance, just in case. Then why don't you have a passport in that junk drawer that's otherwise overflowing with spare batteries and Band-Aids?

Even if you possess MacGyver-style ingenuity, you can't rub together all those bits of flotsam and jetsam to jettison in and out of the country if a "just in case" situation becomes a necessity. A passport, no matter what Boy Scouts may say, is the ultimate tool of the prepared. Practically speaking, it is less bulky than stockpiles for the next big disaster and can accommodate all types of unknowns, from pleasant surprises to worst-case scenarios. **If you take a wrong turn off of the New York State Thruway and end up on the Canadian side of Niagara Falls, a passport enables a trouble-free U-turn. If your honey wants to whisk you away to a European city for the weekend – no problem, you're prepared.** If you win an all-expenses-paid vacation to the Bahamas, you're there.

★ 33 ★

||||||||||||||||||||||||||| NO RISKS, NO REWARDS. >>> REASON No. 7 |||||||||||||||||||||||||||

Now, what other emergency precaution has the power to deliver fond memories, as well as souvenirs for the mantel? Definitely not a hurricane kit.

Still not convinced of these optimistic daydreams? If you fancy yourself more of an escape artist than a roaming romantic, a passport suits your personal arsenal. Nagging parents, the long arm of the law or alien invasions might be the dramatic start to your long-fantasized transformation from average citizen to border-jumping outlaw. In order to join a roving gang of spies, no-goods and playboys, you'll need a valid passport, because a grocery-store discount card and your driver's license won't get you much farther south than San Diego.

Once you've invested in a sexy blue passport, the fancy cars and political intrigue will all come later, we promise.

I need a passport in case I meet a HANDSOME STRANGER who wants to whisk me away to PARIS at a moment's notice.
— ERIN C, CALIFORNIA

IIII FLYING ACROSS OCEANS? NO TIME! >>> REASON No. 8 IIIIIIIIIIIIIII

LOVE IT or LEAVE IT

>>>>>>>>><<<<<<<<<<>>>>>>>>><<<<<<<<

American citizens are lucky. Those who leave are not exiles but expatriates – living outside our homeland is a choice, rather than a necessity. Dissatisfaction with the status quo has long propelled successive generations abroad. The gaudy Gilded Age drove painters like **James McNeill Whistler, Mary Cassatt** and **John Singer Sargent** into the arms of bohemian Paris. Another wave of artists stormed the European continent after WWI. The so-called Lost Generation (including **Ernest Hemingway, John Dos Passos** and **ee cummings**) found, in Europe, liberation from the American commercialization of the 1920s. African-American jazz musicians emigrated to Europe for racial equality – a freedom not available in America. Ironically, these historical malcontents were more instrumental in securing America's place in the international art canon than many of the country's loyalists.

REASON No. **6**

C'MON, LIVE A LITTLE

AT SOME POINT, AMERICANS TURNED AWAY FROM BEING A NATION OF PIONEERS AND EXPLORERS and became a country-size version of the trapdoor spider, which spends its entire life underground waiting for the world to come to it. When it detects motion overhead, the spider pounces from its hiding place and, with lightning speed, grabs its meal. Then it retreats back into its lair, uninterested and even fearful of the world beyond.

Like the spider, you too could burrow deep into a routine, never leaving your hometown and never wondering what is over the next hill. Some people call this stability. But everyone knows that it is the precursor to boredom or, worse yet, provincialism. Even the most devout homebody occasionally feels the inevitable onset of cabin fever. "Before it's too late," the distant glow on the horizon might whisper, "c'mon, live a little."

Traveling might seem like the opposite of nesting, but they often go hand in hand. Our own country, for example, was settled by those with a serious bent for adventure. Religious asylum seekers, struggling farmers and explorers with an unfettered frontier spirit leapt over ponds and continents to find a better life, or just to see what was on the other side. Even Uncle Sam continues to exploit our national travel bug with the slogan "See the World," intended to lure new military recruits away from the security of their childhood homes.

Somehow all this exploring hasn't created a country populated by Peter Pan wanderers unable to grow up or settle down, as their mothers might have warned. Instead, our immigrant ancestors have cultivated such a comfortable society that we've become unrepentant couch potatoes. Apparently, Americans only wanted to travel when the going was tough. The hardships of a month-long passage across the Atlantic aboard a cramped steamer or a dangerous cross-country journey in a covered wagon seduced, rather than deterred, the crowds.

Now that jet travel has evaporated distances and economy class is luxurious compared to Calistoga wagon trains, isn't it time to reclaim our gypsy beginnings? Step up and seize your birthright as a passport-carrying citizen, and make one of those frontier-bound ancestors in your family tree real proud.

"Having kids shouldn't prevent people from traveling overseas, in fact, they make it more fun by noticing things that we would never see on our own."

– RHONDA P, CALIFORNIA

TOP 10 THINGS YOU CAN'T FIND IN YOUR BACKYARD >>>

There's no denying that America's purple mountains are indeed majestic, and those fields of grain do look like amber waves. But some of the world's more bizarre and wonderful sights aren't contained between our shining seas. Poke around the globe, and discover these unusual phenomena:

1. Tropical fruits that look like hairy tennis balls (SOUTHEAST ASIA)

2. Lizards the size of small dogs (MALAYSIA, INDONESIA, and CENTRAL AMERICA)

3. Motorcycles delivering cartons of eggs stacked 3ft high (SOUTHEAST ASIA)

4. Water buffalo plowing a muddy rice paddy (SOUTHEAST ASIA)

5. Cheese shops that are supposed to smell like armpits (EUROPE)

6. Monkeys stealing laundry from a clothesline (INDIA)

7. Cantinas with built-in urinals in front of the bar (LATIN AMERICA)

8. Embalmed Communist leaders on public display (RUSSIA, CHINA and VIETNAM)

9. Equal-opportunity moustaches – they aren't just for men anymore (EASTERN EUROPE)

10. Real-life shepherds with the crook and all (INDIA)

7

IT'S NOT SUCH RISKY BUSINESS

TERRORISM! CRIME! MONTEZUMA'S REVENGE! SCARY PEOPLE WHO SPEAK STRANGE LANGUAGES! Is that why you, like many other Americans, have confined yourself within our cozy borders?

Maybe these statistics will help put things in perspective. Besides having the most violent crimes per capita of any developed nation, the US also is reportedly home to over 75% of the world's serial killers. And although terrorism exists in different forms around the world, the risks are surely higher in the US than in Tahiti or Iceland.

Take a look at travel insurance, and you'll notice that it's awfully cheap. That's because insurance companies are willing to bet big bucks that your fear of traveling abroad is greater than any real risk. Concerns about illness from food, water and insects can be easily combated by a quick pre-trip visit to your doctor, plus bottled water and a reasonably discriminating diet. The greatest danger abroad is the same as at home: traffic accidents.

If you go looking for safety problems in other countries, you'll surely find them. But there are just as many relaxed and hospitable places abroad where the residents don't bother to lock their doors and where people regularly invite even perfect strangers to stay in their homes. When's the last time that happened in Cleveland?

Not feeling safe enough yet? A passport helps to ensure your security by guaranteeing your access to the hundreds of US embassies and consulates abroad. These agencies proudly state that they are "a home away from home" for US citizens (although they probably prefer that you don't plan on spending the night) and can help if you run into problems. If you really want to play it safe, you can pre-register your travel itinerary online with the State Department (https://travelregistration.state.gov/ibrs). That way, Uncle Sam will know where to track you down in an emergency.

Much of the worry about international travel comes down to our basic human fear of the unknown. But once you take that first step to venture abroad with your passport, you'll see that most of the planet is a normal, friendly place. And you'll never look back.

FIVE ADVANTAGES OF HAVING A US PASSPORT

> Many countries waive visa requirements for US passport holders.

> You're eligible for citizen services from US embassies and consulates abroad.

> A passport is indisputable proof of your identity and citizenship.

> You'll always be prepared if you need to leave the country on short notice.

> And you can always come back home again, without any friction or fuss.

40

TOP 10 SAFEST COUNTRIES

>>>
1. **NEW ZEALAND**
2. **GERMANY**
3. **SPAIN**
4. **ITALY**
5. **UNITED KINGDOM**
6. **CHILE**
7. **CANADA**
8. **AUSTRALIA**
9. **CZECH REPUBLIC**
10. **FRANCE**

AND WHAT ABOUT THE US?
IT CURRENTLY RANKS 27TH, RIGHT AFTER ARMENIA.

ISN'T IT ABOUT TIME?

YOU'RE AN AMERICAN, SO ODDS ARE THAT YOU'RE GOING TO LAST ABOUT 77.6 YEARS ON EARTH. With all of life's obligations – 2.07 children, a mortgage, a career and maybe an alimony or two – that doesn't give you much time to get out there and see what's happening on this planet of ours. You may think of international travel as a luxury only available to those with more vacation days and more money to burn than yourself.

With today's discounted airlines and direct flights, travel abroad doesn't require many more resources than a road trip to a neighboring state. Driving from St Louis to New Orleans sounds like a reasonable journey, right? You probably wouldn't give the distance or time it takes a second thought, if you wanted to go to Mardi Gras. But in the same amount of time, you could fly to Brazil for Rio's Carnaval and experience a celebration that's five times the size, with twice as much sunshine and half the clothes.

If you live on the East Coast, the flight to Western Europe lasts just a bit longer than a plane ride to the West Coast. Take your pick between San Jose, Spain, or San Jose, California – it's virtually the

|||||||||||||||||| LET'S ESCAPE TO THAT TROPICAL ISLAND. >>> REASON No. **11** ||||||||||||||||||

same flight time. If your heart's desire is roomy beaches and warm waters, consider boarding a quick flight to tropical San Jose, Costa Rica, or scenic San Jose (del Cabo), Mexico. For more of an unadulterated cultural experience, try San Jose (de los Llanos), Dominican Republic.

Although conventional wisdom tells us that 72 hours is 72 hours whether you spend it in Tacoma or Timbuktu, it doesn't always feel that way. **A week in Paris, France, will be more memorable than a week in Paris, Texas, or Paris, Maine.** All you need to do is slow down and soak up the atmosphere abroad. A precious week or two of vacation time spent in another country can really seem as full as a month-long trip, or a lifetime.

Hurry up, get your passport and get out there – the clock's ticking.

In Around Five Hours or Less You Could...

1 Drive from New York to Virginia...
or fly to **Jamaica**

2 Drive from Chicago to Detroit...
or fly to **Mexico**

3 Drive from Los Angeles to Las Vegas...
or fly to **Costa Rica**

4 Drive from Miami to Orlando...
or fly to **Peru**

5 Drive from Houston to New Orleans...
or fly to **Ecuador**

" Every moment of your time abroad seems
more intense and valuable. Things that are
boring at home – like public transportation,
grocery stores and soap operas – all take on
new and interesting significance as windows
into another culture. Even the plumbing's
fascinating. Time spent in another country
is worth every little second."
– TOM B, COLORADO

BEFORE I DIE, I WANT TO DO SOMETHING HISTORIC. >>> REASON No. **31**

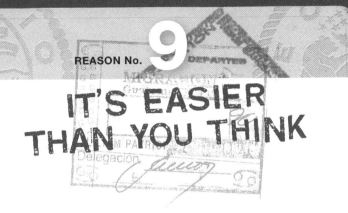

IT'S EASIER THAN YOU THINK

ONCE UPON A TIME, IF YOU WANTED A HAMBURGER, YOU HAD TO HUNT AND KILL A COW, carve it up, then cook it over a fire built by rubbing two sticks together — a complicated and time-consuming process, to say the least.

International travel used to be stuck in that caveman age. You had to rely on a travel agent to pre-book every detail of your flights, hotels and rental cars (and you could only choose from a limited pool of options). For cash, you had to lug around a wad of traveler's checks, then find banks overseas to convert them.

Thankfully, we have pulled ourselves out of the tar pits. Provided your trusty passport rests at your side and you have a credit card and Internet access, planning and executing a trip around the globe are as easy as ordering a burger from McDonald's.

Full-service travel websites are a good place to begin; you can make reservations for trains, planes and automobiles (plus lodging and tours) all at the same site, with a few simple clicks of a mouse. Or you can surf to local vendors' websites. **Need to fly to Bora Bora? Search Air Tahiti's site. Want to confirm a place**

ISN'T TRAVELING ABROAD KINDA RISKY? >>> REASON No. **7**

to sleep in Bangkok? Email a reservation straight to the Buddy Lodge Hotel. Desire a car? Log on to a US-based rental company site; nearly all US rental agencies have international offices, so you can arrange for a Fiat in Brazil or a Volkswagen in Germany to be ready and waiting.

The ease continues once you reach your destination. In Provence, for instance, the stone castles and lavender fields whizzing by the window aren't the sights you're used to seeing, but the highway you're driving on is like any American road, with big green signs and gas station exits. Need cash? Mosey up to an ATM, slip in your everyday bank card and voilà – out squirt Euros, pesos or shekels. Hungry? At any restaurant – be it in Reykjavik or Omaha, food, drink and a table to sit at are always on the menu.

It's all so navigable. When armed with patience and a passport, the rapids of the whole wide world are easy to paddle.

✳   ✳   ✳

"Traveling abroad is surprisingly low-hassle.
I think people underestimate how much
it is like flying to someplace within the USA."

– WILLIAM L, KENTUCKY

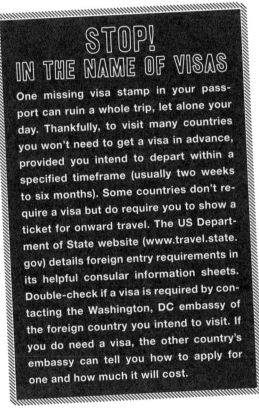

STOP!
IN THE NAME OF VISAS

One missing visa stamp in your passport can ruin a whole trip, let alone your day. Thankfully, to visit many countries you won't need to get a visa in advance, provided you intend to depart within a specified timeframe (usually two weeks to six months). Some countries don't require a visa but do require you to show a ticket for onward travel. The US Department of State website (www.travel.state.gov) details foreign entry requirements in its helpful consular information sheets. Double-check if a visa is required by contacting the Washington, DC embassy of the foreign country you intend to visit. If you do need a visa, the other country's embassy can tell you how to apply for one and how much it will cost.

IIIIIIII I NEED TO PINCH THOSE PENNIES WHEN I HIT THE ROAD. >>> REASON No. **10** IIIII

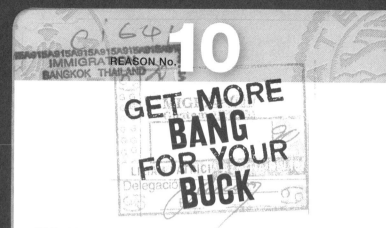

GET MORE BANG FOR YOUR BUCK

FOR SOME REASON OUR FAMED YANKEE INGENUITY CAN FORGE SEMICONDUCTORS OUT OF CLOTHESPINS but fizzles out when it is time to plan a vacation. Our inherited knack for innovation merely resigns itself to a mediocre domestic weekend that costs as much as a monthly car payment. An overpriced hotel room blocks from the beach, and a few crummy seafood dinners, is what we call relaxation on a wage-slave's budget. So get yourself a passport and book a trip overseas, where the almighty US dollar may be strong enough to catapult you from poverty to privilege.

Let's do the math: a daily trip budget in New York City will hover around $150 to $200 for a starving artist's existence, rather than Donald Trump-style luxury. Now pan to the other side of the globe, where a mere $25 a day goes a long way on a tropical island, say, in Thailand. Settle into a beachfront bungalow, sip sunset cocktails, feast on a seafood barbecue dinner and enjoy a traditional massage for those tired sunbathing muscles. After the third drink, you might grow giddy about the Land of the Free, whose hulking currency entitles you to live it up in these blissful places.

|||||||||||||| I'VE GOT THE BLING-BLING ALREADY, BUT NO TIME TO SPEND IT. ||||||||||||
>>> REASON No. **8**

> **❝**I live more frugally overseas because I realize how very little I really need.**❞**
>
> – **STACEY M**, SAN FRANCISCO

Then, of course, even if you visit pricier destinations, you won't need to spend much for certain intangible goods, like experiencing a foreign culture (even if you just laze beside the hotel pool) or bragging to your friends. **Honestly, which sounds better: "We just got back from Tahiti" or "We just got back from Panama City...in Florida"?** Honey, you've moved beyond kiddie-church-camp vacations. And here's a little secret: in foreign countries you can bargain for knock-off designer fashions. That means cheap just got cheaper.

But what about those international flights, which cost nearly twice as much as domestic trips? Don't fear, burgeoning globetrotters. A quick draw of the calculator shows that a daily budget in paradise will soon counterbalance the increased airfare. And what about the hefty application fee for a passport? If you break down the cost over the passport's 10-year lifespan, it's less than 3¢ per day. Mere pocket change can transform your penny-pinching budget into a veritable trust fund. Now that's smart money.

TOP 10 BARGAINS OVERSEAS

>>>

FREE	1. Turtle-watching in **Costa Rica**
FREE	2. Exploring Paris' atmospheric **Left Bank**
$2	3. Riding a camel in **Morocco**
$2	4. Feasting on a three-course meal in **Peru**
$10	5. Skiing in **Slovakia**
$15	6. Sailing around the scenic islands off **Croatia**
$20	7. Buying a designer handbag in **Hong Kong**
$20	8. Admiring Cambodia's star turn, **Angkor Wat**
$50	9. Taking a jungle tour into the **Amazon**
$100	10. Scuba diving in **Thailand**

★ 50 ★

IT'S
ALL
ABOUT
YOU

★★★

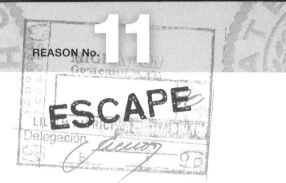
ESCAPE

WHEN LIFE HANDS YOU LEMONS – A HEART-SPLINTERING BREAKUP, KIBOSH-ED JOB, APARTMENT TURNED CONDO – TO HELL WITH MAKING LEMONADE. Grab your passport and break loose.

Distance is the best balm for battered souls. When it comes to healing all wounds, it's faster-acting than time, and way more fun. Who can remain sad or mad when rocking back and forth in a hammock? The sun has just set on your holiday island, leaving behind an abalone sky flecked with iridescent bits of midnight, violet and molten red. For a split second you think about home, then you take a pull on your beer and dodge a coconut falling from the jewel-toned sky. Home schmome.

Technically, you could find a pretty good place to string up a hammock in the 50 states. Here's the problem, though: See that lady by the palm tree? She reminds you of your boss. And that smug (but handsome!) bastard at the bar? Looks like your ex. Egads, now your cell phone is ringing. Doesn't your mom understand you're on vacation?

You've got to put an ocean or two between you and your stressors to escape all the way. The backdrop can be anything – a megalopolis, a one-horse village or the aforementioned island – as long as it's far away

★ ★ **52** ★ ★

from home and a far cry from your daily routine.

Do the unusual: **fly-fish, soak in a thermal pool, seek enlightenment under a banyan tree, shop for a tailor-made suit, bobsled down a mountain, eat breakfast at noon.** When out-of-the-ordinary activities mesh with distant locales – from Tahiti to Tokyo, the outback to Ouagadougou – a power-packed double whammy of rejuvenation results.

Another perk to a great escape is, it stirs up envy. Friends will admire your audacity upon departure and your serenity upon return. Foes (ex-boss, ex-spouse, ex-anything) will stomp their feet in disbelief that you made the dash for the border.

So the next time life serves you lemons, make a Singapore Sling. That's right – chuck the lemons completely and go with something sweet, new and exotic instead, compliments of your passport.

taking the cure

Ever since Roman times, when folks with names like Marcus or Laetitia would seek out the healing waters of specially designated baths for their R&R, people have traveled for health reasons. By the 19th century international health tourism had exploded, notably at European spas near thermal hot springs and at sanatoriums high in the mountains.

Many such places continue to reinvigorate visitors today. With your passport you can sip the 43-mineral spa water in Bath, England; soak away arthritis and muscle aches in the bubbling, geothermal (and sulfur-stinky) waters of Rotorua, New Zealand; or even clear up psoriasis at the springs near Sivas, Turkey, where "doctor" fish nibble away affected skin (said to cause a pleasant tingling sensation).

> "It's always important to have your passport ready so you can take advantage of cheap last-minute airfares and make a quick getaway!'
>
> – JULIANNA V, CALIFORNIA

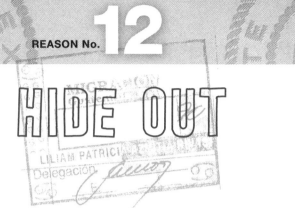

HIDE OUT

LONG THE PROVINCE OF OUTLAWS AND THE RICH AND FAMOUS – **think Butch and Sundance holed up in Bolivia, or Jackie O well shaded in Jamaica** – hiding out is accessible to any Jane or Joe Schmoe with a passport.

With that little blue book, you reap the pizzazz and international intrigue that comes with lying low in Rome or the Riviera. Without it, you're relegated to going underground in Des Moines or Cincinnati. Not sexy, plus not very effective if it's anonymity you crave.

It sounds illogical, but just see what happens if you turn up in Milwaukee and try to disappear for a few weeks. People buzz around you: "Where are you from? What's your business? How long are you staying?" Turn up in Zurich or the south of France, and no one cocks an eyebrow.

Being far from home, in a different culture, allows you to behave more dangerously. You might talk to strangers, order a martini shaken not stirred or belt out a Tom Jones or Carly Simon tune at the karaoke bar. In the motherland you'd shy away from such pursuits, for fear of running into your boss or fifth-grade teacher or someone else who has

★ 55 ★

a preconceived notion about how you should act. In Brisbane or Baden Baden? Not a chance, and that frees you to step into a different skin.

Tie a silk scarf around your neck, light up a cigarette and be a café sophisticate in Paris. Grow a rugged patch of stubble, don a fedora and be Indiana Jones in Tangier. Are you a mild-mannered, early-to-bed accountant in Boston? Stay out all night clubbing in London. Perhaps you fancy yourself a writer, but that part of your character gets masked beneath your day job as an executive assistant. Overseas, you can carry around a notebook and fill it with scrawl. "Are you a writer?" someone will inevitably ask. Smile and nod. The more you say it, the more you believe it.

It seems odd, but it's true: by hiding out, the real you may reveal him/herself.

❝ Being away from home, I can become someone different; maybe a more ideal version of myself appears. It lets me explore who I want to be. **❞**

– **JANE L,** NEW YORK

The King of Hiding Out

LADIES AND GENTLEMEN: Elvis Presley left the building on August 16, 1977, but perhaps not for that Great Stage in the Sky. According to many fans, Elvis faked his death at Graceland, slipping out to start a new life away from the pressures of fame and from white jumpsuits tight as sausage casings. He's been spotted worldwide, from Berlin (eating an extra-large pastrami on dark rye in a deli) to Toronto (singing karaoke in a bar) to London (riding a double-decker bus near Marble Arch). Further sightings, more recently reported by the faithful on www.elvissightingbulletinboard.com, include Tel Aviv, Israel; Wellington, New Zealand; and Winnipeg, Canada. Alas, without the sideburns and fried peanut-butter-and-banana sandwiches, such sightings are difficult to verify.

FIRE UP YOUR SEX APPEAL

HERE'S THE THING: YOU HAVE A VERY THICK ACCENT. It's screamingly evident in the way you tickle those R's with your upturned tongue and let your O's and I's glide, flat and slippery, to the back of your mouth. It's an American accent, and it's going to follow you wherever you go, regardless of whether you're speaking English or Swahili. It's unconscious. It's inescapable.

It's also outrageously sexy.

Let me explain.

A passport is your ticket to a global party, one where love-starved Australians and Swedish hotties are thrown together in a simmering stew of international romantic intrigue. Attachments are low, flirtation is high and no one is averse to a vacation fling (or love connection) that they can juicily recount to friends back home.

This is where you and your accent come in. Because even though you just got your passport, you aren't some hapless newcomer to this transnational booty-shake. No, you are stepping on the scene preceded

||||| BEFORE I FLIRT, I NEED TO GO ON THAT "PASSPORT DIET." >>> REASON No. 15 |||||

by 50 years of unimpeachable American sex appeal. From Nike shoes to Hollywood stars to rock 'n' roll, the groundwork has already been laid, and your accent will mark you as the de facto bearer of this enviable allure.

Does it matter that you don't personally know Beck, or don't exactly resemble Angelina Jolie? Not in the slightest. Because you're going to do something that the stars could never match: you're going to travel thousands of miles just to be at that beachfront bar in Santorini, or the sweaty nightclub in Prague. You are going to the party. And if you combine that dashing American accent with a rudimentary knowledge of world culture, you're going to be a hot commodity indeed.

What's equally exciting, international travel increases your attractiveness once you get home. Think about it. Who would you rather get to know better: a person who spent their summer exploring the whirling dervishes and fairy chimneys of Cappadocia, or someone who spent their summer exploring the Frappuccino menu at the local Starbucks?

Me too, my friend. Me too.

> **"I met my true love five years ago on my first trip to Europe. I went for fabulous clothes, and came back with a leather jacket and a husband!"**
>
> **– DOMINGA R, CALIFORNIA**

A WORLD OF
Romantic Overtures
FIVE HANDY, DEVASTATINGLY POWERFUL PICK-UP LINES
FOR THE TRAVELER ON THE GO

NORWEGIAN Deres vintere er lange og vanskelige. Se på meg som om jeg var et søtt fjell-dyr som ved å komme til fjordene fremskynder våren.	"Your winters are long and miserable. Think of me as a cute mountain mammal whose arrival near the fjords portends an early spring."
ITALIAN Hai mai visto le mani d'un americano farsi romane?	"Ever see an American's hands go Roman?"
SPANISH La salsicha es pequeña, pero picante.	"This sausage is small yet spicy."
SWISS Chum, hoer doch uuf mir dere gschpillte Neutralitaet, darf i nid es Konto eroeffne i diim Haerz?	"Let us cast away pretenses of neutrality! Permit me to open an account in the bank of your heart?"
FRENCH Sans vous je ne suis qu'un paysan.	"I am nothing but a peasant without you."

BE VOTED MOST POPULAR

YESTERDAY, YOU WERE DATELESS FOR YOUR BEST FRIEND'S WEDDING, uninvited to your coworker's birthday party and chosen last for the neighborhood dodgeball team. Today, you are surrounded by admirers and number one on the Date Parade. Was it an Oprah makeover or lottery jackpot win that caused the reversal of fortune? Try a passport, the quickest way to rocket out of the wallflower realm and into the celebrity stratosphere.

Yes, the unthinkable often happens abroad: you – schlubby little ol' you – receive star treatment. You don't look a lick like J. Lo, but villagers in India or the Gambia are staring pie-eyed, admiring your hair and hanging on like paparazzi as you walk to the community tap to brush your teeth. Red hair, pale skin, hairy arms or 6ft height – what's ordinary at home turns heads on distant shores. That's how a geek boy in Albany starts scoring like a quarterback after a quick hop over the right pond.

Some perks of fame: Townsfolk present you with gifts (maybe not Oscar-caliber goodie bags with cashmere pajamas and mink eyelashes, but excellent **souvenirs like local sweets, woven bags, wood carvings, bamboo whistles and stone-inlaid rings**). Handsome strangers in flowing robes ask for your hand in marriage (Arab and Mediterranean countries are particularly rich in offers). Local celebrities invite you to sup with them (it's impossible to get near world music diva Cesaria Evora at venues like Carnegie Hall, but run into her in her hometown of Mindelo, Cape Verde, and she may invite you to her house and serve up beers). Or maybe you're so prominent yourself that people will actually buy tickets to watch you sleep (as has been known to happen in Nepal's mountain villages, compliments of enterprising guesthouse owners who let villagers peek in for a price).

Popularity is all it's cracked up to be when it's grounded in curiosity, generosity and deeply rooted customs of hospitality and cultural exchange. A passport takes you well beyond the usual 15 minutes of fame. It even works in reverse upon returning home, where only you have been to Paris or Peru, and you're voted most popular all over again.

TOP FIVE PERKS OF INTERNATIONAL POPULARITY

> Free dinner and drinks (often in a local home)

> Gifts galore

> Hobnobbing with famous people

> Marriage proposals

> Front-row seats for festivals and events

★ 62 ★

ERIC: MAN OF MALATYA

MY PARTNER, ERIC, ALWAYS WANTED TO BE A ROCK STAR, AND FOR THE THREE DAYS WE SPENT IN MALATYA, TURKEY, HE WAS TREATED LIKE BRUCE SPRINGSTEEN AT A JERSEY UNION HALL.

IN THE MARKET, THE CHEESE VENDOR LEAPT OVER THE COUNTER AND DRAGGED ERIC INTO HIS SHOP, STUFFING HIM WITH GOODIES. THE SPICE VENDOR INSISTED WE COME INTO HIS PLACE FOR TEA. THE BREAD GUYS, DONUT VENDORS, CIGARETTE SELLERS – ALL WANTED ERIC TO SIT, HAVE A CHAT AND TAKE A PHOTO WITH THEM. THE CARPET VENDOR INVITED US TO HIS HOUSE FOR DINNER. SOON, EVERYWHERE WE WENT, LOCALS WERE MOBBING US, SHOUTING, "ERIC!" WHY? PERHAPS BECAUSE FEW AMERICANS TREKKED TO THIS CITY IN TURKEY'S FAR EAST, AND CERTAINLY NO OTHERS WHOSE NAME TRANSLATED INTO "PLUM" IN TURKISH.

THE REAL TEST OF POPULARITY CAME ON NEMRUT MOUNTAIN. ERIC WENT HEAD-TO-HEAD WITH THE TURKISH VERSION OF REGIS PHILBIN, WHO HAPPENED TO BE SIMULTANEOUSLY VISITING THE SITE. SURE, THE TV STAR WAS SURROUNDED BY ADMIRERS SNAPPING PHOTOS. BUT GUESS WHO DREW THE BIGGER CROWD?

– KARLA Z, OHIO

SHIP OUT AND SHAPE UP

A FEW EXTRA TWINKIES DOWN THE GULLET AND SUDDENLY ZIPPING UP YOUR JEANS REQUIRES THE CONTORTIONS OF A CHINESE ACROBAT.

What to do? Books spill off the shelves promising svelteness. *The South Beach Diet? Dr Atkins' Diet Revolution? Dr Phil's Ultimate Weight Solution?* Forget those tomes. The best book for the job is the little blue one titled Passport.

When you travel internationally, a variety of weight loss principles join forces: You don't have a fridge to reach into for butt-widening snacks. **Meals become a deliberate, unhurried affair, not gobbled by the fistful at a desk or in the car.** Portion sizes are smaller abroad – and often more healthy than our super-size fast-food routine, because they are fresh-cooked versus prepackaged.

You'll also get more exercise abroad. You'll walk long distances to explore a destination's famous sights. You'll engage in out-of-the-ordinary activities, like biking up a hill to visit a vineyard or snorkeling out to a coral reef. Heck, mixing exercise and travel is an industry. Several companies and nonprofit groups offer tours that, for example, focus on hiking or biking back roads from Ethiopia to Bhutan, while others arrange sea kayaking trips through the South Pacific.

★ 64 ★

Add to improved eating habits and increased exercise a touch of Montezuma's Revenge – nothing serious, just a day or two of gentle colon cleansing – and you have the makings of the Passport Weight Loss Plan. Unlike Atkins et al, the Passport plan won't deny you one bite, but rather indulge you all the way home – which is where you'll return rested, cultured and able to fit into those American blue jeans, courtesy of other lands.

Diet Fads of the Future
Effective weight loss plans we've tried overseas:

The Himalayan Plan (NEPAL)
Hike up and down 12,000ft mountains for 10 hours daily. Breakfast and lunch: a dwindling supply of trail mix. Dinner menu varies, but may be one bowl filled with either: a radish and ramen noodles, pumpkin and rice, lentils and rice or two Ping-Pong-ball-size oranges.
Average weight loss: 10lb per week.

The Ballpark Diet (SENEGAL)
Peanuts and beer for five days. This is the diet that most vegetarians in West Africa find themselves on.
Average weight loss: 7lb

The Coca Leaf Revolution (BOLIVIA)
Long used by indigenous people in the Andes, the leaves of the coca plant dull hunger, boost energy and soothe altitude sickness.
Average weight loss: 1lb per day.

IIIIIIIIIIIIIIIIII NOT ANOTHER MIRACLE FACE CREAM. SHOW ME THE IIIIIIIIIIIIIIIIIIIIIIIIIIII
FOUNTAIN OF YOUTH. >>> REASON No. 18

REASON No. 16

BUILD YOUR RESUME

IMAGINE THAT THE DREAM JOB YOU'RE HOPING FOR HAS COME DOWN TO JUST TWO CANDIDATES. But only *you* **are able to tack on a humdinger in your interview like** "Well, yes, I spent last summer producing programs on American music for Moscow radio" or "I stayed two months in Guatemala, teaching English to Mayan children."

Suddenly the frontrunner shifts from the candidate with impeccable student body vice-presidential credentials to you and your passport. Working abroad not only sounds good to employers, it shows off that you're able to adapt to new and even flat-out unusual working environments. It's definitely more fun than a "regular" vacation to Disneyworld.

It's easier than you might think, too. With a little creativity, any trip overseas offers fodder for your resume. An advertising major can clip ads in Berlin or Hong Kong to show international awareness back in the classroom. An archaeology student can volunteer at a dig site in Mexico or Egypt. A Web designer can drop by a Laotian Internet company and offer a suggestion, or take one. Small steps abroad look bigger back home.

How? For one thing, you speak English, and a lot of the world wants to. Many developing countries lack proper schools or the money to fund education. Travelers often can add a week of volunteer teaching to a trip around Latin America or Southeast Asia. **With some experience under your belt, you can get paying jobs. In Vietnam private English-language schools often hire travelers to teach eight-week courses, sometimes putting them up in apartments and paying a couple hundred dollars a month, which is far more than you'll need for rice noodles, French-press coffee and a scooter to ride around.** Other international organizations offer teacher training and find jobs for you – all before you leave home.

Of course, the road inspires everyone to write: postcards, long-winded emails, travelogues and online travel blogs. Those looking to cut their teeth in the world of writing can find outlets in English-language papers overseas, which are often starving for product from native speakers. Hey, how do you think we Lonely Planet writers got started?

★ "I had to take a number of trips to London last year while I was working on a case in British court (yes, the Queen's counsel still wear wigs). I took advantage of the opportunity to visit family in Ireland. A lawyer friend was asked to go to Europe for work at the last minute, but she didn't have a passport so she couldn't go. She was bummed."

– JOE H, MINNESOTA

IIIIIIIIIII MY SPANISH WON'T GET ME ANY FARTHER THAN SAN DIEGO. IIIIIIIIIIIIIIIIIIIII
>>> REASON No. **24**

International Office Space

time in:	time out:

About one in 25 Australians pick up their paychecks abroad. An EU passport lets a Brit pick olives in Greece without worrying about a work visa. Working abroad is so common in Europe, students in Britain have a phrase for it: a "gap year." Meanwhile, professionals call getting some distance from their red-faced, screaming boss a simple ol' "career break."

Americans are way behind in the overseas job chase, but you don't have to be. Many organizations help arrange longer-term work visas (which are otherwise tricky to get in Europe and other places). You can farm the Australian outback, tend bar in London, punch lift tickets at a Swiss ski resort or nab an internship in Hungary. Most programs last anywhere from a couple months to a year, and fees run $750 to $1500 – but the experience is worth it, and the income will more than pay off your investment (in most cases).

IIIIIIIIIII I'LL WORK FOR FREE, AS LONG AS IT HELPS SOMEBODY. >>> REASON No. 51

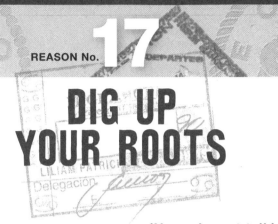

DIG UP YOUR ROOTS

WHERE DID YOU COME FROM? (No, we're not talking about storks and eggs here.) It's basic, human curiosity to want to know your origins. And unless you're Native American, the answer to that question lies buried in the landscapes and lifestyle of another country.

If America is the finish line, where did your family start from? They might have been here for centuries or only a generation. Spin a globe in your hand, let your fingers land on the place where it all began, and you'll feel an inescapable pull. You might have heard your grandparents' stories and wondered what it would be like to walk on Ireland's rocky shores or in the medieval streets of Prague. Why not go see it for yourself?

America is a melting pot, and you should taste the original ingredients. Whether that's oranges from Sicily or the spices of India, try the flavors of "home" for yourself. Feel the winds of the African savannah on your face, or let the musical rhythms of the Caribbean move your feet. Savor the view of the mountains in Vietnam that your

family left behind. A journey to the old world can open up a whole new world for you.

It's one thing to trace your genealogy in dusty library archives or to plot your family's maiden voyage on a map. It's another thing entirely to stand in the place where your ancestors were born and to see that old world with brave new eyes. Then go a step further and show up on a long-lost cousin's doorstep just in time for tea.

A passport can take you in new directions as it teaches you about the old ways. After hanging out on a branch of your family tree in Brazil, you'll want to learn *capoeira*. Just back from Europe, you'll eat blintzes at your local Russian-American cultural society, or write the history of your Jewish immigrant neighborhood. Perhaps you'll find a strange new fondness for the resonant twangs of an Indian sitar. (Hey, it could happen!)

With your passport, the age of exploration isn't over. In fact, it's just beginning.

* * * * *

"In another country, I love to visit the historical sites and walk the very same roads and paths that people hundreds of years ago did, wondering what life was like for them."

– **MITSIE O,** CALIFORNIA

||||||||||||||||||| I WANT TO BE THERE WHEN HISTORY GETS MADE. >>> REASON No. **31** |||||||

A Million Points of Arrival

Off the southern tip of Manhattan under the torchlight of the Statue of Liberty, Ellis Island (www.nps.gov/elis) was once known as the "Gateway to America." The first federal immigration station opened there in 1892, when officials welcomed a 15-year-old Irish girl, Annie Moore, by giving her a $10 gold Liberty coin. In 1907, the station's busiest year, more than one million immigrants took their baby steps into the New World here. It's estimated that half of all Americans today can claim at least one family member among the huddled masses processed via Ellis Island. Curious? Search for passenger records of your own grandparents or great-grandparents online at www.ellisisland.org.

FIND A FOUNTAIN OF YOUTH

IF YOU THINK TRAVEL IS SOMETHING TO DO BEFORE YOU HAVE CHILDREN (and not after), think again. As anyone who has ventured overseas will tell you, lots of young families are out there seeing the world and sharing incredible experiences.

Rest assured, there's no minimum age requirement for getting a passport. In fact, the younger the kid, the better the passport photo. Any kid whose pudgy cheeks or gap-toothed smile graces an official US passport is just too cool for school. A child's first passport is a prized keepsake – and it's even better if it has a few immigration stamps in it.

Children are geared for travel from the moment they start to enjoy stories about Tin Tin and Madeleine. They are blessed with curious minds and are capable of observing the subtlest cultural differences. They delight in new flavors of ice cream, outrageous street entertainers, the unusual sounds of emergency vehicles and novel toys. They learn quickly, picking up new languages even faster than adults. Best of all, their enthusiasm is infectious. Experiencing these thrills pulls a family together in ways that visiting the local shopping mall will never manage.

As small goodwill ambassadors, kids are a lot of fun to have

EVERYDAY STUFF IS FASCINATING – WHEN YOU'RE IN ANOTHER COUNTRY. >>> REASON No. **22**

> **"**Traveling allows me to experience things – and **the more things I experience, the better person I become. "**
>
> – **MATTHEW G**, age 7, CALIFORNIA

along on the road. **In many countries, local people are more likely to take an interest in travelers who have children – there's a universal connection.** At the sight of small American kids, indifferent strangers break out heart-warming smiles and make an effort to connect.

A child's wonderment rubs off on parents, to be sure, but even if you don't have squirts of your own, you will feel younger at heart while traveling. With your passport, it's never too late to rejuvenate. That long-gone excitement you felt when you first left your parents' home returns. You're learning basic skills: how to count the money, how to order a cup of coffee, how to find your way back to the hotel. Everything is more difficult, but somehow it feels good. Forgotten instincts are starting to kick in again. Food tastes not just different, but better. Street scenes sparkle. The hum of humanity is so real. You're taking an interest in everything – just like when you were a kid.

An unexpected perk When Jenny and Russ Wiltse of Denver, Colorado, had their son, Gabriel, they didn't waste much time before getting the little tyke his passport. He was only eight months old. "His passport picture was hilarious," says Jenny. "He looked like a little Mafia baby. Very serious and bald."

Traveling with little Gabriel had unexpected advantages. At border crossings, during passport checks that sometimes can be tense, Russ would show Gabriel's funny passport photo to the guards and almost always, he says, the normally dour-faced guards would crack a smile.

SEEK YOUR OWN HIGHER POWER

DID YOU KNOW THAT QUEEN FRONT MAN FREDDIE MERCURY WAS A ZOROASTRIAN? For those of you who have actually heard of Zoroastrianism, did you know that it was the first monotheistic religion – the forerunner of Christianity, Judaism and Islam?

While our own country is predominantly Christian, the planet teems with thousands of different and lesser-known faiths. Consider the fact that there are more Buddhists and Confucianists than American citizens. There are more Rastafarians than residents of Boston.

At least once in your life you should visit a non-Christian country. Yes, Christianity (in all of its forms) is the world's largest religion, estimated at two billion adherents, but there are some 6.5 billion people on Earth. Islam claims 1.3 billion followers, Hinduism has at least 900 million, Buddhism nearly 400 million, Sikhism around 23 million and Judaism about 14 million – to name just a few faiths.

Non-Christian religions tend to hold different views of existence, birth, death, family, destiny and time, all concepts that you may take for granted. When you travel abroad, be an amateur anthropologist and take some time to compare another religion to your own. You'll

★ 75 ★

> "Whether you are of a **religious, spiritual or scientific frame of mind,** traveling in a foreign environment **strips away many of your preconceived notions** and works as a catalyst for continually **broadening your perspective.**"
>
> **– MATT H**, TEXAS

come to appreciate the surprising number of similarities, and learn a lot from the differences.

It's one thing to read and hear stories about the ancient history of your religion. It's something else to see, hear and touch its living history. **Whether you take a trip to Jerusalem, the Vatican, Mecca or Tibet, a firsthand experience is beyond compare.** While traveling, you can also observe the many ways in which the same faith is practiced across the globe: pay a visit to Christians in South India, Hindus in the Caribbean or Jews in East Africa.

If you consider yourself more spiritual than religious, there are just as many reasons to travel. Find your focus doing yoga in India, or mellow out with tai chi in China. With your passport in hand, you may discover your own higher power while hiking in the Himalayas, surfing sands in the Namib Desert, whooping it up at the World Cup or just savoring Swiss chocolates.

Five Religious Experiences Worth Having

1.
EL CAMINO DE SANTIAGO PILGRIMAGE IN SPAIN
(Catholicism)

2.
DIWALI, THE FESTIVAL OF LIGHTS, IN INDIA
(Hinduism)

3.
THE MONTH OF RAMADAN IN PAKISTAN
(Islam)

4.
VESAK CELEBRATIONS OF THE BUDDHA'S LIFE IN THAILAND
(Buddhism)

5.
CHRISTMAS IN BETHLEHEM
(Christianity)

EXPERIENCE
IT
FOR
YOURSELF
★★★

MEET THE NEIGHBORS

JERRY AND KRAMER. LUCY AND ETHEL. THE FLINTSTONES AND THE RUBBLES. The Kramdens and the Nortons. Having a good relationship with your neighbors is essential, as you probably already know. They can be your best friends, especially in a time of need.

Get out there and meet the people around you – and we don't just mean on your street, in your town or even in our own country. The US isn't an island. With 21st-century communications and transportation, places as far-flung as Japan, New Zealand, South Africa and Chile are all our global neighbors now.

By meeting these neighbors, you'll realize there are overwhelming similarities between people regardless of nation or culture: students are students, surfers are surfers, and shoppers are shoppers. Take a look at the differences, too. Contemplate not only why other people act the way they do, but why you act the way you do.

Remember Sallah and Short Round? Wherever he went, Indiana Jones always had a local sidekick. He was no fool – making friends from other cultures not only grants you deeper insights into the places

you're visiting, but it also helps immeasurably if you run straight into trouble (even if it's not as harrowing as the Nazi villains or Indian death cults chasing after Indy). When you next travel abroad, your new friends might help plan your trip or even host you in their homes.

While on the road, you'll also meet other travelers from across the globe, all sorts of folks liberated from their usual social roles and united with each other by their shared passions. Strike up a conversation – you might discover a common interest in anything from Manchester United to meditation, from oil painting to opera, from politics to pet peeves.

It can also be nice just to meet another American abroad. That person could be an actual neighbor that you've passed on the street back home, and yet you've never had the occasion to chat with him or her. You never know – you could come back with a new best friend, business partner, love interest or even a partner for life.

" Only by visiting another country do I have the opportunity to meet people from foreign lands, all while enjoying the beauty of their native surroundings amid hundreds (or thousands) of years of culture. It's the thrill of using all of my senses at one time – seeing and hearing people go about their everyday lives, smelling and tasting food at an open-air market and touching works handcrafted by local artisans – that makes visiting other countries essential for me. **"** – DAN B, ILLINOIS

IIIIIIIIIIIIIIIIIIIIIIIII ACTUALLY, I'M KIND OF A HOMEBODY. >>> REASON No. **42** IIIIIIIIIIIIIIIII

THEY'VE GOT US SURROUNDED!

Entries

THE US BORDERS ONLY TWO COUNTRIES: MEXICO AND CANADA. BUT MOST NATIONS HAVE MANY MORE NEXT-DOOR NEIGHBORS THAN WE DO, AND MORE CONTACT WITH OTHER CULTURES.

* by way of Russia's satellite state of Kaliningrad

ARGENTINA	PARAGUAY	BOLIVIA	PERU	COLOMBIA	VENEZUELA	GUYANA	SURINAME	FRENCH GUIANA	URUGUAY

BRAZIL BORDERS 10 OTHER COUNTRIES

BELGIUM	LUXEMBOURG	GERMANY	SWITZERLAND	MONACO	ITALY	SPAIN	ANDORRA

FRANCE BORDERS EIGHT OTHER COUNTRIES

RUSSIA	MONGOLIA	NORTH KOREA	KYRGYZSTAN	TAJIKISTAN	AFGHANISTAN	KAZAKHSTAN	PAKISTAN	INDIA	NEPAL	BHUTAN	BURMA (MYANMAR)	LAOS	VIETNAM

CHINA BORDERS 14 OTHER COUNTRIES

FINLAND	ESTONIA	LATVIA	BELARUS	UKRAINE	AZERBAIJAN	GEORGIA	KAZAKHSTAN	MONGOLIA	NORTH KOREA	NORWAY	CHINA	POLAND*	LITHUANIA*

RUSSIA BORDERS 14 OTHER COUNTRIES

★ 81 ★

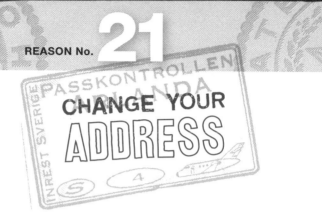

CHANGE YOUR ADDRESS

IT'S A COLD, DREARY JANUARY MORNING. The alarm clock rings. You groan and burrow deeper under the covers, not wanting to face another day stuck in a classroom or at the office. Instead, you imagine yourself lying on a tropical beach somewhere, gazing at the waves and being fanned by warm winds. You long to break your routine, to escape to a warmer, more festive climate and to investigate new cultures and lifestyles. You desire a change of address.

We've all got a dream destination tucked away in our heads. Maybe it's a terraced villa overlooking the sunny Mediterranean, with the surf breaking gently below. Or maybe it's a rustic cabin hidden deep in the snow-covered Canadian Rockies. Perhaps you desire the vibrant energy of a busy Asian metropolis. Wherever the location of your fantasy, you know it can be yours if you just take that first step. Then, with a passport in hand, all you have to do is go.

Living overseas is a mind-altering experience. Not only can you learn a new language, but you can also come to appreciate things you've always taken for granted. Your self-confidence will increase, and you'll

|||||||||||||| A QUICK GETAWAY IS JUST THE THING FOR ME." >>> REASON No. 11 ||||||||||||||

find yourself looking at situations in ways you've never done before. In fact, immersing yourself in another culture can be one of the most vital things you'll ever do.

There are countless ways to make that big international move. Interested in working overseas? You could be an IT consultant in the developing world, a teacher at a US embassy school or a freelance foreign correspondent. What about volunteering internationally, maybe even for the United Nations? For the academically inclined, there are thousands of study-abroad programs.

Home stays are another way to involve yourself in a foreign culture. You'll live with a local family and learn the ins and outs of daily life, as well as make some new friends. Do you like the sound of that but want a bit more independence? Arrange a house swap with someone from another country, and truly live like a native.

Opportunities like these to find a home away from home are endless and only limited by your imagination, not your zip code.

★ 83 ★

My first trip abroad was to Taiwan in the early 1990s to teach English. I knew little about Taiwan except that the residents spoke Chinese, which I didn't, and that the language barrier alone would induce serious culture shock. Still, I applied for a passport and left with only $500 in hand. Within two weeks, I had found a job working at a small English school, was studying Chinese and had a lovely rooftop apartment that swayed in the breeze. I loved the anarchy of Taipei: the seedy bars, the modern apartment houses and the smoky, incense-filled temples. I also developed an enthusiasm for Chinese art and literature, interests that spurred me onward to a graduate degree and a writing career.

– **JULIE G**, UTAH

FIVE WAYS TO MAKE THE FIRST MOVE

> Teach English in Japan

> Rent a castle in Germany

> Study Spanish in Mexico

> Volunteer at a refugee camp in Thailand

> Buy a summer home in Belize

IIIIIII I NEED A WHOLE NEW LIFE, NOT JUST A NEW ZIP CODE. >>> REASON No. **52** IIIIII

FEEL THE THRILL OF THE (UN)FAMILIAR

IF LIFE HAS BECOME TOO ROUTINE AND YOU LONG TO SAVOR EACH MOMENT, then a passport is the Vita-meatavegamin you've been looking for. When you're in a far-flung corner of the Earth, you'll find yourself taking an interest in all those little details of your day that, at home, you simply take for granted.

Waking up in a strange land is an event filled with excitement and uncertainty. The light is of a different hue, the air feels new on your skin and the sounds coming in through the window tell you that you are somewhere you've never been before. You might be awakening at the crack of dawn to the noise of roosters crowing and bicycles rattling down a bumpy dirt road, or voices calling in a new language while a rousing song crackles out of a tinny speaker.

You set out with a list of sights to see, but walking down the street makes you just want to roam. You want to stick your nose into hardware shops, where jumbled assortments of buckets and tools and ladders look unusual rather than mundane. Or maybe the sight of old men getting their shoes shined in the plaza makes you feel content to claim a park bench and soak it all in. **The mannequins in shop windows look like dated rejects from American department stores, but they are attired in saris or tunics or flowing Vietnamese pantsuits cut from exotic fabrics. People are washing their clothes by hand – huh, people still do it that way?** You have to learn how to cross the street by wading through a swarm of bicycles, motorbikes and cars, all without the benefit of a stoplight – who'd have thought you'd have to learn how to do that? It's scary and thrilling at the same time.

When you travel to new places, your days are jam-packed with memorable observations and revelations. You're aware of all the little sensations that fill each minute. Time slows down a notch. You feel more alive. And your passport will be the magic little booklet that makes it all happen.

* * * * *

"My favorite part of visiting another country is the pleasant disorientation and confusion that comes from being in an unfamiliar culture and city."

– BRETT A, CALIFORNIA

STRANGE NIGHT ON THE MEKONG

MY FIRST NIGHT IN THE MEKONG DELTA, I WOKE UP IN THE MIDDLE OF THE NIGHT AND COULDN'T REMEMBER WHERE I WAS. HEARING THE SOUND OF BOATS KNOCKING EACH OTHER ON THE DOCK OUTSIDE REMINDED ME THAT I WAS IN VIETNAM. I WAS ALERT BUT CALM, AND I LAY STILL UNDER MY MOSQUITO NET. I BECAME AWARE OF QUIET MUSIC BEING PLAYED ACROSS THE RIVER, BUT IT WAS UNLIKE ANY MUSIC I'D EVER HEARD BEFORE. A WOMAN WAS SINGING A MELANCHOLY SONG, BUT AS HER VOICE CARRIED OVER THE WATER, IT TOOK ON A SLIGHTLY DISTORTED AND HAUNTED QUALITY. MY EARS BECAME ATTUNED TO THE LOW VOLUME, AND HER VOICE SEEMED TO BEAM DIRECTLY INTO MY HEAD. IT WAS LIKE A TIN-CAN TELEPHONE. I LISTENED, MESMERIZED, DEEP INTO THE NIGHT.

– TOM D, CALIFORNIA

RIDE PLANES, TRAINS & RICKSHAWS

REMEMBER BEING FASCINATED BY TOY CARS, TRAIN SETS, HORSES, GARBAGE TRUCKS, PONIES and just about anything else that moved when you were a kid? Don't be ashamed to admit those sorts of things still get you going. Whether you're eager to test-drive the newest Porsche, photograph classic vehicles as they age gracefully in the back alleys of Buenos Aires, ride the world's fastest bullet trains or lope around on camel back, you'll be grounded without a passport.

Here at home there are strict laws governing the quality of vehicles allowed on the road. So you'll be amazed by what constitutes motorized transport in some foreign places – often little more than two axles, a few tires and a steering wheel. (In fact, you may come to appreciate our automobile emissions standards and not feel so cranky about your next smog test!) The favorite way to get around in Thailand, for example, is a motorized tricycle, known as a *tuk-tuk*. These speedy menaces take turns at daredevil speeds, cough up clouds of blue smoke and are irresistible to travelers.

Driving around a foreign country is convenient, but it limits what you see and it can be a rather solitary experience. Cozy up to locals by riding the densely packed chicken buses in Guatemala, the reggae buses on Caribbean islands or the dusty transport trucks in Mozambique. Or travel by bicycle or rickshaw – you'll slow down and get to know the place better. More traditional means of getting around, such as canoes, camels, elephants and donkeys, will transport your imagination to another era, as you fancy yourself a daring adventurer.

Transportation abroad is not just quaint, either. **You can see amazing natural sights while in transit on Peru's high-altitude trains, in mountain jeeps in the Himalayas or on Caribbean island-hopper flights.** You'll also find high-tech public transit systems and vehicles that will impress and astound you. Witness the punctuality of the Danish train system, the posh high-speed catamarans zipping between Hong Kong and Macau, and the Ferraris, Maseratis and Lamborghinis twisting on roads through the Italian mountains.

Now, those are some toys that any adult can be proud of.

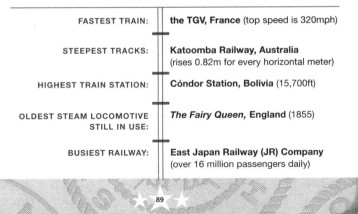

GLOBAL TRAINSPOTTING

FASTEST TRAIN:	**the TGV, France** (top speed is 320mph)
STEEPEST TRACKS:	**Katoomba Railway, Australia** (rises 0.82m for every horizontal meter)
HIGHEST TRAIN STATION:	**Cóndor Station, Bolivia** (15,700ft)
OLDEST STEAM LOCOMOTIVE STILL IN USE:	*The Fairy Queen,* **England** (1855)
BUSIEST RAILWAY:	**East Japan Railway (JR) Company** (over 16 million passengers daily)

ABOVE THE ANDES

Forget about the Space Needle, the Sears Tower or the Empire State Building. It's airplanes that have the ultimate observation deck. I grew up in Seattle and was always impressed by the size of Mt Rainier. Towering over the city skyline, it's the highest peak in the continental US. When I first traveled to Argentina, the flight stopped in Santiago, Chile, and then crossed the Andes Mountains to Buenos Aires. The view over the Andes from the airplane is one of my most enduring memories from a trip full of them. Not only were the mountains larger than Rainier, they made up an entire range running practically from horizon to horizon. No need for crampons, ice picks, carabiners or Sherpas – it was the perfect way to see the full breadth of the Andes, all from my window seat.

– **THOMAS K**, WASHINGTON

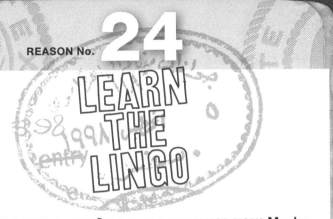

LEARN THE LINGO

***HABLA USTED ESPAÑOL? PARLA ITALIANO? NON?* Maybe it's time to learn.** Getting a passport and traveling overseas gives you an opportunity to break out of your linguistic rut and enter more adventurous tonal territory. By speaking with locals in their own tongue, you clearly send a message (even as you stumble over pronunciation and break all of the grammatical rules) that you're sincerely interested in their way of life and want to meet people on their own terms.

Forget Mark Twain's old adage "Better to remain silent and be thought a fool than to open your mouth and remove all doubt." On the road, that advice won't get you far, and you'll miss out on that humorous chat with your Mexican cab driver or a lively exchange with the French-speaking postman in Timbuktu.

When words fail, pantomiming and sign language can help you get your point across. Just keep in mind that not all gestures are universal. For example, the "Okay" gesture (a circle formed between the tips of forefinger and thumb) commonly used in North America is considered obscene in some Latin American countries. In France, it

IF I SPEAK A LITTLE THAI, DO YOU THINK MY TUK-TUK DRIVER WILL SLOW DOWN? >>> REASON No. **23**

might mean "zero" or "worthless." In Japan, it's asking for a bribe.

Sometimes the funniest and most memorable travel moments occur when communication breaks down. **Perhaps while sitting in a Barcelona café you order a *jabón* (soap) sandwich instead of a *jamón* (ham) sandwich.** Could you ever forget the amused look on your waiter's face, not to mention the curious smiles from diners at other tables? Or, what if in Stockholm, you intend to strike up a *samtal* (conversation) with a new friend but instead suggest that you *samlag* (sleep together)? At the time, the embarrassment will be cringe-worthy, but you'll have a terrific story for the folks back home.

In any tongue-tying situation, remember to smile – it will help you leap over even the most formidable of language barriers. And that advice goes double for your passport photo.

Ĉu vi parolas Esperanton? ┆ Do You Speak Esperanto?

At the end of the 19th century, a Polish ophthalmologist named LL Zamenhof constructed an international language that he hoped would promote peace between people of different ethnic and linguistic backgrounds. He published his work under the pseudonym Doktoro Esperanto ("Doctor Hopeful") and, thus, the language of Esperanto was born. The Esperanto movement caught on quickly, and it's estimated that there are now over

Now You're Talking!

DANISH

Hvor er den nærmeste rutschebane? >>> Where's the nearest roller-coaster?

DUTCH

Ik ben uitgegleden over een bananenschil. >>> I slipped on a banana peel.

INDONESIAN

Maaf, Nona. Ada bebek di atas kepala anda. >>> Excuse me, Miss, there's a duck on your head.

LATIN

Si hoc legere scis, nimium eruditionis habes. >>> If you can read this, you have too much education.

TURKISH

Lütfen bana pantolonunuzu verin. >>> Please give me your trousers.

two million speakers worldwide. Esperantists claim that the language's simple grammatical construction and phonetic spelling system (one letter = one sound) make it easy to learn. Literature and even films have been created entirely in Esperanto, the most memorable being the 1965 film *Incubus,* starring an Esperanto-speaking William Shatner who battles to save his soul from a beguiling tunic-clad demon.

25
THE EWWW! FACTOR

YOU'VE HEARD THE INTERNATIONAL FOOD AND TOILET HORROR STORIES, and you're concerned – it's understandable. Let's discuss the dreaded scenario up front.

You sit down at a busy café. You can't read the foreign-language menu, and after some confusing charades with the waiter you simply point to #23 and nod your head. (FYI: It will be days before you find out #23 translates into "ram's testicles pickled in whey and pressed into a cake.") Because you're gulping a jug of wine to ease the meal's passage, nature soon calls. The waiter points out back to a dilapidated hut with a latch door, beside which various farm animals nuzzle. The mighty stench signals it isn't a place to linger over a good book. As for toilet paper...well, you'll have to get creative.

Yuck, right?

The funny thing is, the more you journey, the more you'll be thankful to travel's "ewwws" for the way they enhance its "aaahs". Think of the sweet-mash whiskey scent in the air over the Scottish highlands. Or the taste of fresh-split coconut milk on a Thai beach. Would these "aaahs" be so lofty had they not been preceded by a meal of chopped organ meat boiled in a sheep's stomach, or a 6-inch beetle gnawing on your toes?

ACTUALLY, I'VE GOT SOME LOFTIER TRAVEL GOALS IN MIND.
>>> REASON No. 29

Granted, it's rocky at first. Let's call that Stage One, where "ewwws" loom large and heighten "aaahs" by contrast (and when indoor plumbing inspires unabashed devotion). As you persevere into Stage Two, the "ewwws" and "aaahs" begin to blend, and "ewwws" lose some of their icky power. **A big, honking camel gob on your shirt fades into insignificance as you ride across the Sahara's coppery dunes. And the noxious smell barely registers as you paddle through raw sewage to reach the inspiring riverside temple.**

We call these character-building experiences, and your passport is a ticket to a big stinky world of them. Ultimately, all "ewwws" turn into "aaahs," and that's when your passport has done its job, broadening your tolerance and sensory boundaries. Next time you visit a village market and find everything equally enthralling – the severed pig's head next to shimmering silks, and the llama fetuses next to fanciful weavings – you'll know your conversion is complete.

TOP FIVE
TOILET PAPER STAND-INS

As used by Lonely Planet authors
and staff in times of urgent need

> Snowballs

> A grassy slope

> Leaves

> Low-denomination bills in a
  foreign currency

> Lonely Planet guidebook pages
  (of course, carefully selected to
  minimize loss of essential information)

TASTES LIKE CHICKEN?
Dishes that are nose-scrunching to some cultures
are lip-smacking to others.

* * * * *

ICELAND SERVES UP *HÁKARL*, PUTREFIED SHARK MEAT, AND *SVIE*, SINGED SHEEP HEAD (COMPLETE WITH EYES) SAWN IN TWO, BOILED AND EATEN EITHER FRESH OR PICKLED.

IN THAILAND PEOPLE EAT LARGE, COCKROACH-ESQUE WATER BUGS BY PEELING OFF THE CARAPACE AND STRIPPING OFF THE LEGS; THE BUGS ARE SAID TO TASTE LIKE SOFT CASHEWS INSIDE.

THE FRENCH ARE EUROPE'S BIGGEST CONSUMERS OF HORSE MEAT. THE OLDER THE HORSE, THE MORE TENDER IT IS – THE OPPOSITE OF OTHER MEATS. IN SOUTHERN JAPAN, IT'S SLICED UP RAW AND SERVED AS BASASHI.

ROAST GUINEA PIG IS A DELICACY IN PERU, WHILE DOG MEAT IS A SPECIALTY ITEM IN VIETNAM (ESPECIALLY IN THE NORTH, WHERE LOCALS BELIEVE ITS CONSUMPTION BRINGS GOOD FORTUNE – BUT ONLY IF EATEN DURING THE SECOND HALF OF THE LUNAR MONTH).

IIIIIIIIIIIIIIIIII I WANT TO FEEL SOME OF THOSE "AHHHS" FIRST. >>> REASON No. 34 IIIIIII

STAY AWAKE IN CLASS

IMAGINE YOURSELF IN THESE TWO SCENARIOS: In the first, you are sitting at home reading a book on Chinese history. In the other, you are actually in China, totally immersed in the local way of life. Your day is spent visiting an 800-year-old temple, exploring an imperial palace, strolling through bustling markets, eating a sumptuous feast of Beijing duck and perhaps finishing off the evening at a colorful opera. Now ask yourself: which scenario gives you a more exciting opportunity to learn about vibrant Chinese history and culture?

Traveling is an education in itself. Having a passport and venturing overseas gives you the chance to witness things that could never be described as vividly in a dry textbook. Politics, history, geography, religion and architecture are brought to life through your encounters with different peoples' traditions. And unlike school, you won't have to force yourself to stay awake to do so – just watching how people interact and haggle in a market, eating the local cuisine and learning about what folks like to watch on television can make for an excellent education. You'll come away from your travels wiser in the ways of the world than you ever thought possible.

Hundreds of learning experiences are offered in every corner of

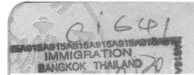

the planet. Wherever you go, you're sure to find ways to study language, the arts, natural science, archaeology or cooking, just to name a few. Academic types could enroll in a formal student-exchange program at a university while dilettantes can seek out any of the more casual short-term options available. **Whether you take a cooking course in Thailand, dart African leopards in the name of conservation research, learn Italian in Italy or study *vipassana* meditation in India,** these authentic, hands-on educational experiences will inspire you, enrich your life and provide you with a treasure trove of fantastic memories.

So don't limit yourself to that armchair! A passport can make all those marvelous places you've only read about leap off the pages of a book into a new hyperreality.

"Travel
is the best education
you could ever receive
no matter what your age."

– LINDA W, CALIFORNIA

IT'S TOO LATE. I'VE ALREADY GRADUATED.
NOW I REALLY NEED A JOB. >>> REASON No. 16

WARMTH FROM WITHIN

I'll never forget the year and a half I spent in a college dormitory in Xi'an, China, studying Mandarin Chinese. I lived with people from all over the world: Japan, Finland, France, Russia, Korea and Australia. Our living conditions were far from satisfactory; the crumbling dormitory was broiling in the summer and freezing in the winter. My fondest memories, though, are of the subzero evenings I spent huddled around a coal furnace with my international roommates playing mahjong and drinking *baijiu,* pungent Chinese rice wine.

Tough times? You bet!

But I'd do it again in a heartbeat.

– JULIE G, UTAH

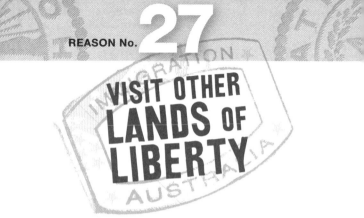

VISIT OTHER LANDS OF LIBERTY

NO JAYWALKING, NO TOPLESSNESS ON THE BEACH, no loud music, no gambling, no bonfires, no drinks served after 2am, no drinking in public, no fireworks, 55mph speed limits, no smoking (tobacco or otherwise) – in many parts of this self-proclaimed Land of Liberty, there are an awful lot of laws governing our day-to-day lives. Sometimes you just wanna have fun.

Abroad, you can find plenty of places that won't meddle as much in your business. We're not talking about lawlessness (which you can find in other countries, too, but isn't necessarily in your best self-interest). We're talking about civilized places where the laws underscore a whole different set of social values. Europe, for example, has lower drinking ages, and there is no such thing as an open-container law there; you can have a beer on the tube in London or on the beach in Ibiza, as long as you're 18 (sometimes even younger).

In many foreign countries, your inner wild child can go topless (or bottomless) on the beach. Smokers don't have to sneak around

|||||||||||||||||||||||||||||||||||||| SO, I'VE GOT THE RIGHT TO LIFE, LIBERTY AND THE ||||||||||||||||||
PURSUIT OF HAPPINESS. AND TRAVEL, TOO? >>> REASON No. 3

like petty criminals either. It's a liberating change to smoke in movie theaters, classrooms or pretty much anywhere else that you can think of to light up a cigarette. In parts of Indonesia, in fact, any man who doesn't smoke is considered suspect.

If sunbathing nude while smoking cigarettes and drinking beer in public is not enough for you, head to Amsterdam or Copenhagen, where you can legally smoke weed – for breakfast, if you like. Even if you choose not to inhale, the fact that people there are not in fear of getting ticketed by the police (or worse) is refreshing. However, make sure to sober up before testing out fifth gear on the speed-limit-less German Autobahn.

BUZZ KILLS

NO GUM OR SPITTING IS ALLOWED IN SINGAPORE.	**ROCK MUSIC IS FORBIDDEN IN BURMA (MYANMAR).**
WOMEN CAN'T DRIVE IN SAUDI ARABIA.	**ALCOHOL IS ILLEGAL IN MANY MUSLIM COUNTRIES.**
IT'S ILLEGAL TO KILL A SASQUATCH (if you can find one, that is) **IN BRITISH COLUMBIA, CANADA.**	

TAKING IT TO THE STREETS

Once when traveling in Brazil, a couple pulled me aside and said, "We have a very serious question to ask you about the United States." Their tone was unnerving, and I assumed that they wanted to know about slavery, segregation, war or something else rather unsavory from our national past. However, they proceeded to ask, "Is it true that you cannot drink a beer on the street in America?" When I told them that it was true except for along the Las Vegas Strip, on Bourbon Street and a few other choice spots where police tend to look the other way, they were honestly upset. To them, drinking in the streets, especially during festivals, was a basic right seemingly on par with the freedom of speech.

– THOMAS K, WASHINGTON

★ 102 ★

EXPERIENCE EXTRAORDINARY EVENTS

LET'S FACE IT. YOU PARK YOUR CAR IN THE SAME SPOT ALMOST EVERY DAY. You already know what's for lunch and where every conversation is going. You need to experience something radically different, something fresh to slip you out of the daily grind.

Of course, there are exciting events taking place all over the US, but – again – you have a pretty good idea of how they're going to turn out: you sip martinis and the ball drops in Times Square, you drink bourbon and watch horses at the Kentucky Derby, and you guzzle hurricanes and throw beads at Mardi Gras.

Isn't it time to cross a border into another country? Go find something that dazzles you anew, blows your mind and leaves you as wide-eyed and exhilarated as a kid. Check out a full-moon party in Thailand or Oktoberfest in Munich. Watch the Tour de France in person. Or gaze at a comet from the top of a Mayan pyramid in Guatemala.

If Halloween isn't quite as thrilling as in your trick-or-treat days, take a trip to see the funeral culture of Toraja in Indonesia, the public burning *ghats* (funeral pyres) in Varanasi, India, or Day of the Dead parades in Mexico. If televised sports and the gym no longer sate your competitive appetites, take off to attend the next Olympics, watch the

Yomiuri Giants host the San Francisco Giants or check out the Grand Prix in Monaco.

Does your mind never stray far from food and drink? You should sniff out truffle hunting and Beaujolais in France, or sample the spicy 11-day Thai Food Festival hosted in Bangkok's World Trade Centre. **When music is a must, don't miss the Roskilde rock festival in Denmark, the Sumfest summer reggae jam in Jamaica, Carnival in Trinidad and Tobago, the Dakar-Gorée Jazz Festival in Senegal or the hundreds of DJs and million-plus revelers at Berlin's Love Parade.** Try celebrating a holiday abroad, too. What's better than a tropical New Year's Eve or a true white Christmas, replete with reindeer, in Finland?

You never know – you could find yourself at the center of an extraordinary event. Don't get left at home without a passport when your garage band tours Europe with a new single or when you need to accept that well-deserved Nobel Prize in Sweden. It could happen.

TOP FIVE NOT-TO-BE-MISSED CELEBRATIONS

> **CARNAVAL**
> in Rio de Janeiro, Brazil

> **DAY OF THE DEAD**
> in Mixquic, Mexico

> **SAN FERMÍN**
> (the running of the bulls)
> in Pamplona, Spain

> **SONGKRAN WATER FESTIVAL**
> in Chiang Mai, Thailand

> **CHINESE (LUNAR) NEW YEAR**
> in Hong Kong

EVERYBODY TALKS ABOUT
THE MAIN **CARNAVAL** IN RIO,
CARNATAL in NATAL, BRAZIL.
but I love A smaller version of Carnaval, it takes place in the northeastern part of the country much later in the year. It isn't such a big commercial event, just a full-on old-fashioned street party with music, drinks, dancers and everything else that makes life worth living."
— BRENDA L, MICHIGAN

|||||| I NEED STORIES TO TELL MY GRANDKIDS SOMEDAY. >>> REASON No. **48** ||||||||||||||

ALL THE WONDERS OF THE WORLD

THE EARLY CENTURIES BC MAY HAVE LACKED TRAVEL AGENTS AND ONLINE RESERVATION BOOKING, but that didn't stop the ancients from journeying to behold spectacular sights — and compiling a tip-top list of the best of the best. Whether celebrated for their richness or extraordinary scale, the original Seven Wonders dropped one's jaw.

That, it turns out, is the hallmark of a Wonder, be it age-old or modern, natural or man-made, personal or universally regarded – it sets the mouth agape.

Take the Pyramids of Egypt, the first Wonder. The largest structure, Khufu (Cheops), was built by 100,000 workers stacking 2.3 million limestone blocks, each weighing $2^{1}/_{2}$ tons or more. A visit today still sparks reverential head-shaking. You'll ask yourself, "How'd they do it?"

While the other early Wonders – the Hanging Gardens of Babylon, the Lighthouse of Alexandria, the Colossus of Rhodes, the Temple of Artemis at Ephesus, the Mausoleum at Halicarnassus and the Statue of Zeus at Olympia – have fallen away, plenty of new candidates have risen to take their place.

I'M PRETTY WONDERFUL MYSELF. >>> REASON No. 12

Do you prefer your Wonders well promoted and populated? Try Cambodia's Angkor, with monkey-guarded temples and spooky stone faces peering out from the jungle, or Peru's Machu Picchu, the riddling Inca city that floats amid mountain-trapped clouds. Then again, maybe you appreciate subtle and isolated Wonders, in which case the megaliths of Scotland's Orkney Islands might please, or the giant stone heads toppled across Nemrut Dagi's peak in eastern Turkey.

Wonders can be wet (a prankish pod of wild dolphins in Kaikoura, New Zealand) or dry (the fat streaks of stars that smudge the night sky over Morocco's Sahara Desert). They can be sacred (Tibet's Jokhang Temple, which maroon-robed monks walk around clockwise, chanting and spinning prayer wheels under clouds of juniper incense) or secular (Jordan's Petra, an exquisite trade-route city carved from sandstone two millennia ago).

Ultimately, a Wonder is a personal pick. So throw the dart north, south, east or west. With a passport in hand, you won't have to wander far before reaching a Wonder.

KARLA Z'S SEVEN WONDERS OF THE WORLD

> Sunrise over the Ganges River, Varanasi, India

> Old Town Square, Prague, Czech Republic

> Nemrut Dagi, Turkey

> Swayambhunath Temple, Kathmandu, Nepal

> Medina of Fes el-Bali, Fes, Morocco

> Street vendors' food, Bangkok, Thailand

> Wrigley Field, Chicago, USA (what do you expect from a hometown girl?)

HOME LOOKS PRETTY DARN GOOD AFTER ALL. >>> REASON No. **42**

ALL THE WONDROUS SPINOFF LISTS
The catchy "Seven Wonders" concept has spawned generations of imitators.

* * * * *

THE SEVEN WONDERS OF THE MEDIEVAL WORLD INCLUDE STONEHENGE (ENGLAND), THE COLOSSEUM (ITALY), THE CATACOMBS OF KOM EL SHOQAFA (EGYPT), THE GREAT WALL OF CHINA, THE PORCELAIN TOWER OF NANJING (CHINA), AYA SOFYA (TURKEY) AND THE LEANING TOWER OF PISA (ITALY). RUNNERS-UP INCLUDE THE FORBIDDEN CITY (CHINA) AND NOTRE DAME (FRANCE).

THE SEVEN WONDERS OF THE MODERN WORLD, ACCORDING TO THE AMERICAN SOCIETY OF CIVIL ENGINEERS, INCLUDE THE EMPIRE STATE BUILDING (US), THE ITAIPU DAM (BRAZIL/PARAGUAY), THE CN TOWER (CANADA), THE PANAMA CANAL (PANAMA), THE CHANNEL TUNNEL (UNITED KINGDOM/FRANCE), NORTH SEA PROTECTION WORKS (NETHERLANDS) AND THE GOLDEN GATE BRIDGE (US). THE ENGINEERS WHO WROTE THE LIST FOCUSED ON 20TH-CENTURY "IT-CAN'T-BE-DONE" TYPE OF STRUCTURES, WHICH EXPLAINS WHY ACHIEVEMENTS LIKE THE TAJ MAHAL (INDIA), KREMLIN/RED SQUARE (RUSSIA) AND THE EIFFEL TOWER (FRANCE) ARE MISSING.

THE SEVEN NATURAL WONDERS INCLUDE MOUNT EVEREST (NEPAL/TIBET), THE GREAT BARRIER REEF (AUSTRALIA), THE GRAND CANYON (US), VICTORIA FALLS (ZAMBIA/ZIMBABWE), THE HARBOR OF RIO DE JANEIRO (BRAZIL), PARICUTÍN VOLCANO (MEXICO) AND THE NORTHERN LIGHTS.

FIND THE TRUTH BEHIND THE FICTION

THE WORLD HAS ALWAYS BEEN AWASH WITH RUMORS. People have been swapping stories – some tall, some true – for as long as language has existed. If you've always wanted to get to the bottom of things, forget the books. Go straight to the source, and travel to foreign lands that have long intrigued you. Your quest may not always bring answers. In fact, it may only bring more questions, but you're sure to reach some profound and surprising conclusions just the same.

You've probably heard a thing or two about the Greeks. Ever wonder about the Oracle of Delphi? You may get all the answers if you run into the ghost of you-know-who near the shrine. Better yet, forget the immortals and head to Athens, via Marathon, retracing the 26-mile journey attributed to a soldier named Pheidippides. According to legend, the young man arrived, breathlessly announced the Greeks' surprise victory over Persia and expired upon the spot. "Rejoice, we conquer" were his final words.

Perhaps you'd rather see the facts behind all the talk of despotic Russian czars. Begin at St Basil's Cathedral in Moscow. Supposedly, Ivan the Terrible blinded each one of his architects after the church's completion so they could never make another building as beautiful. Impossible? See it for yourself.

Maybe you have an appetite for the supernatural and want to visit the birthplace of one of history's most infamous tales. **Start in the medieval town of Sighisoara in Romania, then walk the streets that Transylvania's notorious son, Vlad Dracula, once roamed. Just don't linger after dark.**

Ever wonder about those Old Testament tales of love and betrayal? Now's the time for a trip to the Holy Land. First stop: Asquelon, an ancient city known for its *femme fatales*. Beneath the scorching sun, visualize the day that Samson fell prey to Delilah's charms and lost his strength after receiving an awfully bad haircut (what do you expect from a bunch of angry Philistines?).

With the history of the world being so rich and baffling, the biggest question is where to begin. The answer is easy: with your passport, my fact-finding friend.

HISTORY'S TOP FIVE MYSTERIES

> Stonehenge, UNITED KINGDOM

> Easter Island, CHILE

> The Sphinx, EGYPT

> Tikal, GUATEMALA

> Nazca Lines, PERU

THE ONLY WAY TO KNOW FOR SURE IS TO BE THERE YOURSELF. >>> REASON No. 31

FORGOTTEN BY TIME

The quest for "lost" cities of the world is an endless source of intrigue among archaeologists. One of the most fascinating discoveries of the 19th century was the unearthing of Petra, a once flourishing, 2000-year-old city that lay hidden in a gorge in Jordan until its discovery by a Swiss explorer. Despite its prominence in the first century AD, Petra's monuments, fantastically carved into the surrounding cliffs, lay unseen for hundreds of years. Machu Picchu is another site that stirs the imagination. Hidden deep in the cloud forests of the Andes, the old Incan settlement still baffles archaeologists. Its finely crafted stonework indicates that it was once a vital ceremonial center, although no one knows why it was abandoned long before the Spanish arrived.

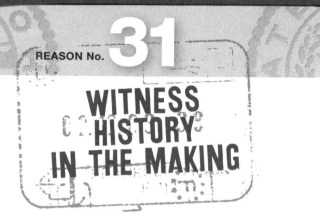

WITNESS HISTORY IN THE MAKING

SOMETIME IN THE EARLY 1920S, IN THE MONTPARNASSE DISTRICT OF PARIS, a young man from Illinois began appearing in La Closerie des Lilas café. He sat at one of the marble-topped tables and spent the day scrawling away inside his blue-backed notebook. As per his usual request, the waiters brought him coffee (no sugar) and let him be, little realizing that this man would one day become one of America's greatest living writers. Ernest Hemingway was just one of many American dreamers drawn to Paris. The city's low cost of living, its abundantly flowing wine casks and its rich cultural heritage brought visitors by the boatload, all wanting to be part of a city on the edge of history.

Today, Paris no longer possesses the same allure it had for Prohibition-era Americans. Yet quiet cultural revolutions keep happening in other corners of the world, and what applied then still applies today: you can read about it after it's over, or instead you can get your ticket (and a passport), see it for yourself and be a part of history.

Imagine being there to witness the collapse of the Berlin Wall, to offer a hand to a young East Berliner as he or she scrambles over the

IIIIII HISTORY ISN'T THE ONLY SUBJECT THAT MAKES MY DAY. >>> REASON No. 26 IIIIII

rubble and breathes for the first time the air of a free city. Or envision taking part in the Velvet Revolution, which transformed Czechoslovakia into a democratic republic. **Picture yourself watching the 2004 presidential elections in the Ukraine, as millions gathered on the city squares and in parks to voice their displeasure at attempts to destroy (with poison, in fact) the pro-Western candidate.**

Of course, politics is only one small part of history. You can also witness the next solar eclipse over Finland, catch fantastical, never-to-be-repeated festivals and visit new nations – like Croatia, a former war zone that is today one of Europe's loveliest destinations. Consider your passport your admission ticket to history's best plays as they unfold upon the world stage. You can hear about it in 10 years' time, or see it now with your own eyes. The choice is yours.

★ 113 ★

TOP 10 PICKS FOR EUROPE'S NEXT "CITY OF LIGHTS" >>>

ETERNAL ROAM

Italy's cultural capital (and the world's capital from 200 BC to AD 348), Rome offers the imaginative wanderer a chance to time-travel. Walking through the eternal city is like peeling back the centuries to the dawn of Western civilization. Start at Palatine Hill, where the city began in 730 BC. Gaze at 2000-year-old aqueducts, then look for ghosts at the Roman Forum, where Julius Caesar's body was cremated following his assassination. Then pick up the trail of Christendom (which began after the city's destruction by Goths in AD 5) **and follow it into the Renaissance, when the world's greatest artists left their mark on the city.** (Incidentally, that's around the time when a certain Italian sailor set off into the unknown, with the dawn of America just a few years away.)

1. **Barcelona,** SPAIN
2. **Berlin,** GERMANY
3. **Budapest,** HUNGARY
4. **Bucharest,** ROMANIA
5. **Istanbul,** TURKEY
6. **Krakow,** POLAND
7. **Ljubljana,** SLOVENIA
8. **St Petersburg,** RUSSIA
9. **Tallinn,** ESTONIA
10. **Vilnius,** LITHUANIA

32

WHERE'S YOUR SENSE OF ADVENTURE?

IN 1271 A TEENAGER NAMED MARCO POLO SET OFF OVERLAND FROM VENICE TO CHINA. One of the first Westerners in the kingdom, he learned the language and served the emperor as a highly valued officer for 15 years.

In 1947, at the age of 33, the intrepid Thor Heyerdahl led an expedition on the balsa raft Kon-Tiki from Peru to Polynesia. Yes, that's right. He sailed a raft right across the Pacific Ocean – simply to prove it could be done.

What have you done with yourself lately?

Everyday people go on extraordinary adventures all the time. There are thousands of lesser-known and unknown adventurers who hail from all corners of the planet. In 1998 a shy Frenchman named Benoit Lecomte swam across the Atlantic Ocean. So, why not you?

Adventure, enterprise and ambition are what brought humankind to the top of the food chain and spread us across the globe. That fact should not be forgotten in our brave new world of car payments, commutes and cubicles. Grab your passport and use your vacation to go on a mission à la James Bond, or find your inner Lara Croft.

IIIII SOMETIMES JUST GETTING THERE IS AN ADVENTURE. >>> REASON No. 23 IIIIIIIIIII

Adventure isn't just for kids. As an adult, you can explore on a grander scale (and afford your own plane ticket). **Sign on for an around-the-world yacht trip, go on a hot air balloon safari in Africa and hike to Everest base camp or even further.** If perfecting your favorite sport or hobby is your mission, you deserve to try it out in the ultimate location. Try fly-fishing in Patagonia or scuba diving off the Great Barrier Reef.

Do you yearn to blaze a completely new trail? Introduce an existing sport to a new environment, as people have done recently with kite surfing off Venezuela. American André Tolmé, for another example, literally golfed his way 1200 miles across Mongolia. These days it's hard to find what Josef Conrad called a "blank space of delightful mystery" on the map, but you can still feel like a pioneering adventurer on some of the back tributaries of the Amazon river, in Antarctica or in the Gobi Desert.

Whatever you do, always seek out a little adventure – or maybe seek out a lot.

"Life is a daring adventure or nothing at all."

– HELEN KELLER

OUTTA THIS WORLD >>>

Space: the final frontier.

Now space travel is not just the realm of NASA and the Trekkie imagination. On October 4, 2004, SpaceShipOne rocketed into the history books. It was the first private piloted spaceship to exceed an altitude of 328,000ft (about 100km) on two successive voyages within 14 days. Ever-adventurous Virgin Group founder Richard Branson is already planning Virgin Galactic, which he hopes will open the doors of private space travel to thousands and "bring alive their dream of seeing the majestic beauty of our planet from above, the stars in all their glory and the amazing sensations of weightlessness and space flight." Before taking this giant leap, you may consider cutting your teeth on a trans-Atlantic flight. At least for the time being, a normal passport should suffice for takeoff and reentry to the planet, too.

Permitted to enter and remain in West Malaysia and Sabah for THREE MONTHS from the date shown above.

|||||| WHERE DOES ALL THIS LEAD TO? I'VE GOTTA KNOW. >>> REASON No. **47** ||||||||||||||

ACTIVATE YOUR LIFE

CROSSING DESSERTS ON CAMELBACK, SWIMMING THROUGH CROCODILE-INFESTED WATERS and scaling sheer rock faces in the Himalayas are several ways to spend a vacation. Or you could spend your holiday flattened on a beach watching the waves roll in as the sun cooks your skin. Yet between these two extremes, there's a whole world out there offering all kinds of activities – trekking through rain forests, biking over rolling Tuscan landscapes, snorkeling with dolphins – that, while not life-threatening, may very well be life-altering.

In your voyage out *there*, you may discover something inside of yourself that you never knew existed, or your travels abroad may ignite a zeal for life that you haven't felt since you were a child. Sure, you can book an activity-filled vacation in the States, but there's something about exotic landscapes mixed with a dose of foreign culture that makes for a magical journey. Besides, the world offers some fantastic settings that you simply can't find at home. And you're sure to have a bit of fun and work up a sweat, too.

You can bicycle across idyllic countryside in Italy, spinning slowly

|||||||||||||||||| FIRST I'VE GOT TO CHANGE MY ADDRESS. >>> REASON No. 21 ||||||||||||||||

past rolling hills by day and reclining outside of picturesque old villas by night (with a glass of nicely aged wine in hand, to ease away the day's strains). Those who prefer the foot to the pedal can walk the lush highlands and unspoiled coasts of Scotland, while enjoying plenty of pub life to boot. Costa Rica and Panama, at America's back door, offer rain forests filled with wildlife, as well as whitewater rafting – if you like your scenery splashing quickly past.

Sea lovers can tan themselves while snorkeling the colorful coral reefs of Belize or southern Mexico.
And, for those who are slow to relinquish the dream of scaling vertiginous peaks, the world abounds with fantastic mountain destinations, including the Swiss Alps, Tanzania's Kilimanjaro or even the Himalayas, which offer trails for experts and novices alike. These are perfect destinations to channel your inner Armstrong – and they may not seem so unreachable once you have that lovely little passport in hand.

FIVE WORKOUTS WITHOUT ELLIPTICAL TRAINERS OR STAIRMASTERS

> Hiking the Inca Trail, PERU

> Kayaking the Chagres River, PANAMA

> Walking the Higashiyama Trail of Kyoto, JAPAN

> Snorkeling coral gardens near Caye Caulker, BELIZE

> Cycling the wine regions of Rioja and Navarra, SPAIN

Before traveling to Peru, the closest I got to mountain climbing was walking the hills near my apartment in San Francisco. I was little prepared for the awe-inspiring size of the Andes. Electricity raced through my veins as Ben and I bumped along dusty roads beneath towering, snow-covered peaks. When the road ended, our four-day trek began. By day we hiked past topaz lakes and Quechua villages as we climbed steadily uphill. At night we cooked our meal and lay out beneath the stars until the cold drove us into our tent. Although it was grueling, I can't remember a time I enjoyed challenging myself more. The Andes certainly whipped me into shape – and gave me a love for mountain climbing I'll never relinquish.

– REGIS S, INDIANA

BANCO CENTRAL DE RESERVA DEL PERÚ

DIEZ NUEVOS SOLES

10

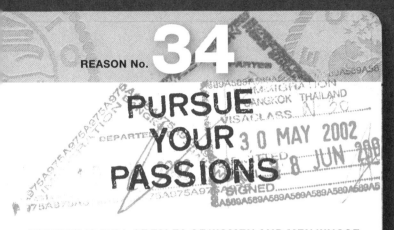

PURSUE YOUR PASSIONS

HISTORY IS FULL OF TALES OF WOMEN AND MEN WHOSE LIVES WERE CHANGED FOLLOWING A TRIP ABROAD. John Keats, Man Ray, Henry James and Gertrude Stein are just a few of the dozens of artists and thinkers who set off in pursuit of what they loved the most, and in their trips abroad ended up changing the course of history.

Following your own passions overseas may not end up altering world history, but it's likely to leave a deep mark on your own life. Whatever it is in this world that moves you – art, music, tropical islands, a fantastic meal – pursue it to the ends of the Earth, and you're always going to return fulfilled.

If art has you fast in its grip, visit the exquisitely wrought universe of Paris' Louvre, or lose yourself in London's British Museum or St Petersburg's Hermitage. Perhaps a particular artist or painting moves you, and you won't be satisfied until you visit the Van Gogh museum in Amsterdam, lay your eyes on the woodblock prints of Hokusai in Japan or prostrate yourself before the fantastic works of Caravaggio in the old churches of Italy.

|||||||||| YOU THINK I CAN GET PAID FOR THIS, TOO? >>> REASON No. 16 ||||||||||

Admirers of architecture can dazzle their senses as they wander through such masterfully carved spaces as Notre Dame in Paris, Gaudi's Sagrada Familia in Barcelona or St Peter's in Vatican City. Istanbul's marvelous skyline and Prague's medieval splendor are likely to inspire you, and if you yen for Zen, head to Japan, where flawlessly maintained gardens and temples will satisfy all your aesthetic cravings.

Those whose interests tend toward the obscure can access a treasure trove of the world's rich arcana by traveling abroad. Philatelists may never be the same once they've gazed upon the astonishing stamps secreted inside the Helsinki Post Museum and those with an eye toward the heavens can turn their world upside down by going on a stargazing journey that begins in Australia—or any other destination south of the Equator.

For fiery souls with many passions: take heart. With passport in hand, traveling to a foreign country is the surest way to stimulate every facet of your being. And if you haven't yet found your greatest passion, there's no better way to discover it than to grab your passport and travel beyond the bounds of your everyday life.

> **"Not to sound shallow, but I love the shopping! It's a tangible way to capture a bit of the culture."**
>
> – DOMINGA R, CALIFORNIA

Bibliophiles Anonymous

When I was a young student, my head was always buried in a book, earning me quite a few unkind nicknames from my peers. Later in life I learned that being a bookworm *and* a world traveler aren't necessarily mutually exclusive activities. In fact, literature has often been my first window into a culture. Strolling the fog-swept Thames at dusk brought me back to the London of Dickens and Conan Doyle, when dark characters roamed the labyrinthine city. Likewise, my first visit to St. Petersburg was less a discovery of Russia than a walk into the shadowy landscape of Dostoevsky's great 19th-century novels. Rome is an inspiring city, but all the more so when retracing the steps of Percy Bysshe Shelley, who wrote his greatest works there.

– REGIS S, INDIANA

|||||||||| FINDING OUT THE TRUTH IS MY PASSION IN LIFE. >>> REASON No. 30 ||||||||||||

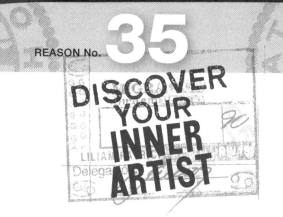

DISCOVER YOUR INNER ARTIST

HEY, WE'RE ALL GUILTY OF IT — THE TRAVELER'S DRIVE-BY. It's something like Chevy Chase's 10-second look at the Grand Canyon in *National Lampoon's Vacation* or the routine at Mt Rushmore: walk back to the viewing platform, get a shot of yourself making the peace sign, then go buy some fudge. And that's okay. But there's something about foreign places — wacky sights, sounds and smells — that flex our observation muscles more strongly. We may find ourselves tempted to linger longer in such a place, perhaps even to pull out a pad and pen and sketch a bit.

In the mid-1800s British writer John Ruskin taught art to everyday folks without regard for the results, believing that the only way to *see* something was to draw it. Ruskin railed against the speed of modern travel; the advent of trains and cameras meant that people — as Alain de Botton put it in his engaging book *The Art of Travel* — paid "less attention to the world than they had done previously."

All right, Ruskin was a bit of an ol' grump, but he had a point: **drawing's good even if you stink at it. A quick sketch**

of a tree, a temple or the wayward hairline of a bus driver takes about 10 minutes, but if you do it, you'll know and remember the scene better. While photos are good memory triggers, too, it'd be a shame to limit your look at the Taj Mahal, Red Square or Sydney Harbor to just the time it takes to press that little button on your pocket camera. Plus, how many of your friends and family really enjoy thumbing through a three-inch stack of snapshots of the great trip *you* just went on?

Art tours are another way to get creative. Many schools and organizations offer international programs that whisk you around places like Tuscany, stopping at Florence's Uffizi Gallery and spending a few hours in a studio to work on your own blank canvas. Often the price is the same as for a vacation, but you'll live like a local and you'll learn something. Plus, if you get famous, you can always sell your napkin doodles sporting real Venetian espresso stains for *thousands.*

TOP FIVE ART BOOKS FOR TRAVELERS

> *The Elements of Drawing* by JOHN RUSKIN

> *Drawing for Dummies* by BRENDA HODDINOTT

> *You Can Sketch: A Step-by-Step Guide for Absolute Beginners* by JACKIE SIMMONDS

> *The Art of Travel* by ALAIN DE BOTTON

> *How to Draw Comics the Marvel Way* by STAN LEE and JOHN BUSCEMA

But Is It Art? When a pal and I traveled up the coast of Vietnam, we decided the bus-to-beach-to-train-to-temple circuit wasn't enough. We'd make our "art film" debut called *Holding Ground Just Beyond the Limits* and travel as character-actors the whole way. In Saigon we had L'EQ (L'Equipe de Québec, or "Québec Team") jerseys made and posed as English-speaking Québecois athletic recruiters scouting talent. Cyclo drivers would stop us on the street ("You play football?" they'd ask). We taped dozens of rehearsed and un-rehearsed scenes – including "speed" checks at a Ping-Pong hall, games of soccer on the beach against skilled locals (overheard: "those guys play like dogs") – and recruited a mustached man from Cincinnati to portray our infuriated boss. In Hue the video cam mercifully broke, with our scribbled-together script only half shot. Alas, the project collapsed. But when we talk of Vietnam, it's mostly about the failed movie.

– ROBERT R, VIRGINIA

La boutique du musée et le restaurant "Le jardin de Varenne" sont ouverts aux mêmes horaires que le musée.

Les toilettes s
Toilets are

RODIN

PLEIN TARIF
5 €

Ce billet ne peut être repris ni échangé.

Per l'achat de ce billet, vous contribuez à l'enrichissement des collections du musée.

EXPO+MUSEE PLEIN TARIF
9,00 Euros

NEO-IMPRESS INDIV.

Le :05-04-05   10:30

Musée Rodin

PHOTOGRAPHY IS MY ART, AND WILDLIFE MY SUBJECT.
>>> REASON No. 37

MOTHER NATURE IS CALLING

REMEMBER ALL THOSE EXCITING SCIENCE CLASSES YOU TOOK IN HIGH SCHOOL? Like that day Mr Jenkins spoke without pause about plate tectonics and oceanic ridges. Wasn't that a hoot!

In reality you may not remember much from that lesson (although you may recall a few strange dreams you had while snoozing through class). But fortunately, as anyone who's gazed into the Grand Canyon can attest, nature in all its unadorned beauty is far more awesome than anything you might have learned from those soporific science texts.

The US has its own natural wonders, but they're just a fraction of the spectacular phenomena awaiting you in foreign parts. If you've ever wanted to watch red lava violently explode in the Ring of Fire, or even fancied peering down into one of those steaming craters, your passport's your ticket. From Central America to Malaysia, you can see dozens of active volcanoes – photograph them, hike them and even enjoy the fruits of these geothermal wonders, like bubbling mud baths in New Zealand and *onsen* (hot springs) in Japan.

|||||||||| DON'T NEGLECT MY SPIRITUAL SIDE, PLEASE. >>> REASON No. 19 ||||||||||

THE EARTH, WILD AND STRANGE: TOP 10 PLACES

>>>

1. **Great Barrier Reef**
   AUSTRALIA

2. **Salar de Uyuni,**
   world's largest salt flats
   BOLIVIA

3. **Rock of Gibraltar**
   SPAIN
   (UNITED KINGDOM possession)

4. **Pantanal**
   world's largest inland swamp
   BRAZIL

5. **Volcán Arenal**
   COSTA RICA

6. **Dead Sea**
   ISRAEL

7. **Himalayas**
   NEPAL

8. **Sahara Desert**
   NORTHERN AFRICA

9. **Lake Baikal**
   world's deepest lake
   RUSSIA

10. **Victoria Falls**
    ZIMBABWE and ZAMBIA

Niagara Falls is charming, but if you want to see some of Earth's most spectacular falls, head to Victoria Falls in Africa or Iguazu Falls in South America. Both are jaw-dropping wonders surrounded by dense rain forest, teeming with wildlife.

For other natural novelties, head to Russia during St Petersburg's "white nights," when the sun never sets, or take a salt bath in the Dead Sea. You can hear symphony orchestra concerts in one of the stalactite-filled chambers of Australia's Jenolan Caves, or test your endurance by traveling mid-winter across Siberia, where the lakes freeze so solidly that Russians once laid train tracks across them. For an even bigger taste of the Ice Age, visit southern Argentina, where the massive blue-hued Perito Moreno Glacier advances slowly eastward, leaving mini-icebergs in its wake today.

Of course, we still haven't mentioned the vast deserts and towering, snow-covered mountains on our big blue marble. These are things you'll just have to see for yourself, all in that wondrous world of science out there.

the wonders of the sky

Turn your world upside down by heading into the deep south – equatorially speaking, that is. Along with wonders underfoot, you'll have a whole different view of the heavens, including the Southern Cross, used by mariners for centuries to navigate a ship's position in the southern hemisphere. Those who want to be dazzled by celestial sights should head to Canada, Iceland or other far northern destinations for premium viewing of the colorful Aurora Borealis (Northern Lights), which occurs in the upper atmosphere when solar particles get trapped in earth's magnetic field. Just don't rely too heavily on a compass to get you home, as all points tend to lead north as you get closer to the northern pole!

WATCH WILD WILDLIFE

SEEK OUT KOMODO DRAGONS IN THE JUNGLE IN IN-DONESIA. Sneak along a ridge on a Rwandan moun-taintop, coming close enough to shake hands with a gorilla. Catch a glimpse of a rare scarlet macaw in southern Be-lize. Climb Himalayan summits in pursuit of an elusive snow leopard. No zoo can compare to encountering wildlife on its own, wild terms.

Even before the dawn of the Enlightenment, explorers roamed the whole world in search of exotic flora and fauna. Marco Polo wrote (if not always truthfully) about the fabled species he found in foreign lands. Centuries later, Victorians went forth in the name of science to find new life hiding under Alpine rocks, in the natural hothouses of the tropics and at cool oases among African sand dunes. Sir Stamford Raffles, founder of Singapore, discovered what is still thought to be the largest flower in the world, the Rafflesia. In 1835 Charles Darwin arrived in the Galapagos Islands off Ecuador aboard the HMS *Beagle*. The diversity of species found thriving there – and nowhere else on the planet – led the young British naturalist to formulate earth-shat-tering theories.

> "As long as I live, I'll hear waterfalls and birds and winds sing. I'll interpret the rocks, learn the language of flood, storm, and the avalanche. I'll acquaint myself with the glaciers and wild gardens, and get as near the heart of the world as I can."
>
> – **JOHN MUIR** (1838–1914), *Scottish-born naturalized American citizen, founder of the Sierra Club*

You don't have to circumnavigate the globe to heed the call of the wild. All you need to do is look out of your hotel window whenever you hear an unfamiliar bird song. Today, eco-adventure tours make it easy to get to remote wildlife-watching hot spots. **You can follow migrating monarch butterflies all the way to Mexico, cross an ice floe to visit a colony of Emperor penguins or get your kicks on a big-game safari in the African savannah** – and take your camera, not a rifle. Chase your wanderlust straight across the Sahara on the back of an ornery but endearing camel.

Your passport is the golden key that unlocks the animal kingdom, a place without borders and where no cumbersome phrasebooks are ever necessary. Meeting the hoofed, beaked and many-petaled inhabitants of another country may make for as many memories as any sojourn among the world's equally diverse and beautiful human kind.

did you know? More than 5000 species of animals and 28,000 species of plants are now protected by the CONVENTION ON INTERNATIONAL TRADE IN ENDANGERED SPECIES OF WILD FAUNA AND FLORA (CITES; www.cites.org), a treaty that first went into effect in the 1960s. More than 160 nations are voluntary signatories, including the US. It's not enough. According to the INTERNATIONAL UNION FOR CONSERVATION OF NATURE AND NATURAL RESOURCES (IUCN; www.iucn.org), which publishes the annual Red List of threatened species, currently about half of all freshwater turtles, one in three amphibians, one in four mammals and one in eight bird species face extinction worldwide.

Motivated to do something about the global biodiversity crisis? THE WORLD WILDLIFE FEDERATION (WWF; www.worldwildlife.org) can help show you the way.

38

TASTE
IS EVERYTHING

WHAT'S ON THE GLOBAL MENU TONIGHT? In Mexico try spicy *mole poblano* and deep-fried grasshoppers, if you dare, washed down with a bottle of fiery tequila. In South Africa you can munch on delicious "bunny chow," a loaf of bread stuffed with savory curry. Fire-ant soup is a big hit in Laos and will (literally) make your taste buds tingle. The sweet mint tea of Morocco is absolutely divine, and dining on roasted camel in Egypt makes a great anecdote for the folks back home.

All the tastes and smells of the native cuisine are among the most tantalizing aspects of visiting a new country. A culture reveals itself through its food, via preparation, etiquette and eating habits. In far-off locales there's nothing like sampling delicacies to give you insight into the ins and outs of daily life there. Everywhere, food draws people together, serving as a focal point for family and friends, for celebrations and social gatherings. Whether you're in a public restaurant or the intimate space of someone's home, breaking bread with the locals is a surefire way to bridge cultural gaps and make lifelong friends.

With a passport the entire world becomes an epicurean

||||||| KIDS LIKE THE GROSSEST STUFF. AIN'T IT GREAT? >>> REASON No. 18 |||||||||||

TOP FIVE EXTREME TASTE TESTS

> Deep-fried monkey toes (INDONESIA)

> Roasted guinea pig (SOUTH AMERICA)

> Pig's blood with scrambled eggs (HUNGARY)

> Barbecued rat-on-a-stick (LAOS)

> Pounded cassava balls *(fufu)* (GHANA)

adventure waiting to be tasted. There are few places on this planet where you'll find yourself at a loss for new flavors and uncommon eating experiences. It doesn't matter if you're eating in a five-star European restaurant or a Vietnamese noodle house – almost every country provides enough gastronomic variety to please the most jaded palate. Wherever you travel, you'll encounter all sorts of weird and wonderful dishes you didn't even know existed.

Of course, "weird" is a relative term: to many Chinese cheese is disgusting, and people from around the world are mystified at America's love of peanut butter. A willingness to try strange and different foods will open up a new world of culinary pleasures to you. Once home, you may even find yourself reminiscing about that tasty squid-ink ice cream you ate back in northern Japan, or thinking fondly of the yak butter tea you shared with villagers in Tibet.

★ 134 ★

"As a foodie, travel has taught me how to drink *mezcal* in Oaxaca, the proper way to construct a *lasagne Bolognese,* that no amount of water can adequately cut the bite of pastis, that deep-fried silkworm cocoons are best eaten in a quick crunch-and-swallow, that piranhas – even freshly caught – really don't taste that good and that there is really something very nice about a simple cheeseburger when I get back home."

– **ADA C,** NEW YORK

☆ THE REAL MONGOLIAN BARBECUE ☆

While living in Mongolia, I once went on a company-sponsored camping trip. Midway through dinner preparations, I asked a coworker what would be the main course, thinking pasta would make for a no-fuss meal. "Coming soon," she said. About 10 minutes later we heard shouts from around a bend. We looked to find some colleagues herding five goats in our direction. "You've got to be kidding me," I thought. The goats were distributed among the various offices, and soon ours was pinned to the ground, its eyes bulging out of its head. Amarbat, a coworker, slit the goat's chest with a knife, slid in his hand and squeezed its heart until it stopped bucking. This was not a particularly appetizing sight, but our furry little friend did make for a tasty meal.

– **MICHAEL K,** CALIFORNIA

IIIIIIII YOU NEVER KNOW WHERE THAT NEXT MOUTHFUL WILL TAKE YOU. IIIIIIIIIIIIIIIIIII
>>> REASON No. **47**

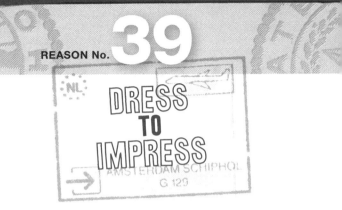

DRESS
TO
IMPRESS

IF YOU FOLLOW FASHION, YOU KNOW THAT TRENDS WASH FROM ONE CONTINENT TO ANOTHER and that many styles originate abroad. Like Uggs, we wish that some styles had stayed where they came from, while we welcome others with open arms and wallets.

If you're into *haute couture*, there's nothing like traveling to the fashion world's fiery inner core of Paris and Milan. You don't even need to visit runway shows to witness how the locals live, eat and breathe fashion. Grab a seat at a café, watch the passersby and determine for yourself whether "burnt pearl" or "dirty yellow" is the hot color for leather handbags this season.

Fashion is not just for those of us who fancy themselves as *glitterati*. Most of the world's threads are of a more casual weave. Don't overlook Costa Rican and Australian surfer chic, South Pacific islander style, the Jamaican Rasta aesthetic, Rio de Janeiro bikini fashion, Austrian snowboarder attire or the *vaquero* (cowboy) look in Mexico. For you guys who claim that you have no interest in clothes or fashion, how cool would it be to have an official South African rugby shirt?

|||||||||| WHO CARES ABOUT CLOTHES? I'D RATHER BE ALL WET. >>> REASON No. 33 ||||

Or suit up in traditional dress for a change. **Choose from kimonos in Japan, saris in India or lederhosen in Bavaria.** You may find a perfect fit. Even if you look ridiculous, at least you won't have to face people at work on Monday. In some places people wear feathers and fur or no clothes at all. Go and spot these peculiar styles, but keep in mind that baseball hats, jeans and athletic shoes may look just as otherworldly to those clad in multicolored feathers.

If you're a shopaholic, you'll be able to hunt down great deals and find fashions that are either hard to come by or are yet unknown at home. Scour the markets, visit a local tailor, peruse the boutiques and make sure that you have extra room in your baggage to haul all the stuff home. As the first person in-the-know, you can say, "I told you so!" when a new style pops up at your local mall.

> **"**Fashion is not something that exists in dresses only. Fashion is in the sky, in the street, fashion has to do with ideas, what is happening.**"**
>
> – COCO CHANEL

And remember, nothing screams sophistication and cosmopolitan attitude like the essential fashion accoutrement: your well-stamped passport.

AN ARTIST'S PALETTE ISN'T CLOTHES, IT'S A CANVAS.

>>> REASON No. **35**

TOP 10 INTERNATIONAL FASHION MECCAS >>>

1. **Milan,** ITALY
2. **Paris,** FRANCE
3. **Buenos Aires,** ARGENTINA
4. **London,** ENGLAND
5. **Tokyo,** JAPAN
6. **São Paolo,** BRAZIL
7. **Hong Kong,** CHINA
8. **Berlin,** GERMANY
9. **Mumbai (Bombay),** INDIA
10. **Barcelona,** SPAIN

"It is not money that makes you well dressed, it is understanding."

– CHRISTIAN DIOR

|||||||||||||||||||||||||||||| IT'S ALL ABOUT FOOD, NOT FASHION. >>> REASON No. **38** ||||||||||||||||||

GROOVE TO THE GLOBAL BEAT

THERE YOU ARE, STANDING IN THE COLONIAL TOWN OF SALVADOR feeling the tropical rays on your face, ice-cold drink in hand and samba playing overhead while an ecstatic group of revelers dances around you. As the drumbeats grow louder, you find yourself caught up in the music, and, try as you might, you just can't keep from dancing. The crowd, the music, and – dare we say it – the alcohol propel you onward. Before you crest the beach, you're in your groove, head over heels in love with this moment, this country, these newfound friends around you.

Just then several thoughts flash through your brain: **"It's February and my friends are freezing their asses off back home," "Deciding to spend Carnaval in Brazil was one of the best decisions I've ever made" and "I'm never going home."**

Music can have a powerful effect on us. It can change the whole mood of a day, make us do rash and stupendous things (like dancing in huge crowds) and carry us into an entirely different frame of mind.

But if you don't travel outside the US, you'll never experience the vast range of musical styles and settings out there. And listening to a few CDs won't do nearly as much to get your feet moving as the intoxicating live rhythms of samba, flamenco, rhumba – or hundreds of other musical styles – rushing through your veins.

The world has a lot to offer in the musical department. Hedonistic revelers should hit the beachside dance parties in Ibiza, where highly vaunted DJs spin eclectic grooves to seriously amped crowds. For a more bucolic experience Montreux is the ticket. The charming Swiss town hosts an eclectic music festival with a lineup of reggae, bossa nova, acid jazz and much more. Other famed festivals take place in the baroque city of Salzburg, the rain forests of Malaysia and even the deserts of Africa.

If an instrument has you smitten, learn from the masters at the source. Travel to India to study the tabla, learn percussion down in Brazil or master the explosive chords of flamenco in Spain. There are bagpipe maestros in Scotland, pan-flute teachers in Peru and even yodeling instructors in Austria. Your passport's your ticket out of a one-note orchestra, and with it you'll never listen to music the same way again.

TOP 10 MUSIC FESTS AROUND THE WORLD
>>>

SOUNDS OF TUVA

1. Montreux Jazz Festival, SWITZERLAND
2. Blues and Roots Music Festival, AUSTRALIA
3. Salzburg Festival, AUSTRIA
4. Glastonbury Festival, ENGLAND
5. Carnaval, BRAZIL
6. Montreal International Jazz Festival, CANADA
7. World Tango Festival, ARGENTINA
8. Rainforest World Music Festival, MALAYSIA
9. World Sacred Music Festival, MOROCCO
10. World Roots Festival, NETHERLANDS

The world is full of musical arts that don't often make top 10, or even top 100, lists. Throat-singing, a complex musical style where the singer produces two or even three sounds (overtones) simultaneously, is a wild but flourishing art in the remote mountain region of Tuva in Russia. Every summer the city of Kyzyl hosts the Khoomei Festival, where the best practitioners of this elusive art come to compete. Paul Pena is one recent American who found his calling in throat-singing. The blind blues musician became smitten with the art when he first heard it on his short-wave radio, and he later traveled thousands of miles to compete in Kyzyl's international festival. You can follow his story in the excellent documentary film *Genghis Blues*. Better yet, catch the festival live in Kyzyl.

ACT LIKE A MOVIE STAR

ADMIT IT, FILM FANS, THE CLASSIC AUDREY HEPBURN MOVIE *ROMAN HOLIDAY* IS A SERIES OF POSTCARDS FROM ROME. The *Lord of the Rings* trilogy is a thrilling advertisement for New Zealand tourism. As we watch these dramas unfold on screen, our eyes are treated to stunning scenery and behind-the-scenes peeks at life in foreign lands. Thousands of people each year have been inspired to board planes so they can cast their peepers on these and countless other cinematic places abroad. With a passport you too can act on that irrepressible desire to walk in Frodo's footsteps. And, like Bogart and Bergman, you and the love of your life can "always have Paris" – but only if you actually go there.

The rewards of traveling are sure to exceed your expectations, because visiting far-off lands is really a hyper-cinematic experience. Your heightened awareness of sights and sounds turns you into a keen observer. But walking the streets of a foreign city is not like sitting with a theater audience; it's more like being the camera. Imagine yourself in Rome, where the over-the-top Italianness of Fellini's *La Dolce*

Vita explodes to life every day. **You're strolling around the Colosseum, panning your gaze along the Via Nicola Salvi, and you spot a Catholic priest, fully attired in robes and a monsignor hat, zipping through traffic on a Vespa.** Before your eyes he pops out in front of a cargo truck, abruptly cuts off several sports cars as he swerves over three lanes, and races by you before zigzagging out of view. That's the sort of exciting moment filmmakers are always trying to capture. But seeing it live is more intense and unforgettable than watching it on the big screen or the boob tube.

Every now and then an international traveler turns a corner to find a film crew at work. This really brings home the cinema-travel connection. Sometimes the crew is short on extras, and it is not unheard of for a tourist to actually step in front of the camera for a small, uncredited cameo. Now that qualifies as an unforgettable twist to your travels.

TOP 10 CINEMATIC SETTINGS

>>>

If the settings of films received Oscars for best supporting actor, surely the following locales would have been nominated:

NEW ZEALAND
(*LORD OF THE RINGS*)

FRENCH RIVIERA
(*TO CATCH A THIEF*)

NEW DELHI (*MONSOON WEDDING*)

TOKYO (*LOST IN TRANSLATION*)

NORTH AFRICA AND ITALY
(*THE ENGLISH PATIENT*)

VIETNAM (*INDOCHINE*)

BERLIN (*WINGS OF DESIRE*)

LONDON (*NOTTING HILL*)

TUNISIA
(*RAIDERS OF THE LOST ARK*)

PARIS (*AMÉLIE*)

TIPS FOR AMATEUR *AUTEURS*

Many people travel with video camera in hand, which, to be honest, generally results in hours of footage that nobody really wants to watch. It's far better to fill your brain with exciting images, rather than commit your memories to two-dimensional video footage. However, if you're dead set on becoming a traveling auteur, here's a bit of advice:

Take the time to learn how to use your camera before you go. Hone some skills first, and you'll get better results when it really counts.

Resist the urge to constantly pan and zoom.

Learn how to edit. Your friends and family will thank you for 20 minutes of cohesive, well-cut filmmaking instead of three hours of random footage.

CHANGE
YOUR
PERSPECTIVE
★★★

HOME SWEET HOME

EVERY YEAR PEOPLE CHALLENGE THOMAS WOLFE'S CLAIM THAT "you can't go home again." In fact, returning world travelers prove him wrong on a daily basis. After spending a few days, weeks or even months in foreign places where everything's a little different, you'll come back home and suddenly relish the simple things, like making a peanut butter sandwich and watching TV or opening mail with your pet turtle, Steve.

Actually, it's an interesting sensation to arrive in your country. Nine out of 10 Americans were born on American soil – and most never leave, thus never getting a chance to feel the thrill of hearing "welcome home" upon re-entering the US, the endpoint for the world's greatest mass migration ever. As many as a million new Americans still reach these shores annually. Today, the first thing they'll see isn't the Statue of Liberty (near New York's Ellis Island), but often an airport immigration desk, just like you.

Not only will you be happy to be home, but you'll look at it a little differently, too. Teens throwing water balloons at your Honda will remind you of the reckless Italian guys pushing each other into 16th-century fountains. The 20th-century Doric columns of your state capitol look like the flourishes on the Parthenon, from the fifth century BC. **Little league games in your neighborhood might bring to mind barefoot soccer games on the graveled streets of Cambodia.**

Maybe ol' Tommy instead should've said that you can't really know your own home, or fully appreciate it, till you've left it. With your passport in your hand, of course.

> ✳ "The thing about going abroad is how
> ✳ much you discover that who you are
> ✳ and where you're from has shaped you.
> When I came home, I settled down
> to a meal of fried okra, potatoes and
> cheese grits. They brought the richness
> of life here back to me."
>
> **– WAMPUS R**, OKLAHOMA

GO BEYOND BORDERS

RECALL YOUR BACKSEAT-IN-THE-STATION-WAGON DAYS, when Mom and Dad commanded the wheel and you were driving to the beach or national park for summer vacation? Remember the shiver of excitement as you crossed into a new state? The signs went by in a flash – "Welcome to Ohio: The Heart of It All" and "Now Entering Kentucky, the Bluegrass State" – but they left you wondering. What exotic things happen in the "heart"? Would Kentuckians be mowing Crayola-blue lawns?

Crossing an international border evokes that same excitement and curiosity multiplied a thousandfold. It's hard to fathom how the simple act of stepping over a line transports you into a new world. The language instantly changes – Spanish becomes French, Turkish becomes Greek. The style of dress alters; women with long, loose hair in Spain might be wearing hijabs in Morocco. The music on the radio flips, say, from tango in Argentina to samba in Brazil. The currency converts, so a Euro in Italy nets 240 *tolars* in Slovenia (you might be a millionaire there!). Laws and religions vary within a few feet one direction or the other. As you stride across that magic stripe dividing two nations, you'll feel like the first explorer, making a grab at the unknown.

A border can be a river, gorge, mountain range or arbitrary divider. It might be sophisticated, utilizing the latest iris-scanning technology, or simple, where you whistle across the stream toward the other country and a guy in a dugout canoe rows over to fetch you, recording your entry into a paper notebook.

Though a border might be carved in stone, it isn't permanent. A skirmish in Eritrea or treaty in Lebanon can move the line overnight. Some borders, like North Korea's, are impassable now, but that will change.

What won't change is the lure of crossing international boundaries once your passport casts its spell. You'll know you've been mojo-ed when you find yourself irresistibly drawn miles out of the way, and you're standing at the threshold of a new country, one well beyond your original itinerary.

Why did the traveler cross the border? To get to the other side, of course.

**TOP FIVE
RUNS FOR THE BORDER**

Countries whose borders are most crossed by tourists, according to the World Tourism Organization (www.wto.org):

> **France (75 million tourist arrivals per year)**

> **Spain (52.5 million)**

> **US (40.4 million)**

> **Italy (39.6 million)**

> **China (33 million)**

SPLITS VILLE

One day in 1944, Soviet troops rolled through a small village straddling modern-day Slovakia and the Ukraine. They quickly put up a fence along Main St, dividing the village in two. The ensuing scene was absurd: people who went to work that morning in the fields on one side of town found they could not return home to their families on the other side that evening – they were now in a different country.

Over the years, the border impacted the quality of life: the Slovak side (now called Velke Slemence) became economically secure as Slovakia joined the EU, while the Ukrainian side (now called Solonci) struggled as part of the post-USSR meltdown.

Villagers who used to be able to walk across the street to each other's homes now must travel 30 miles to the nearest border crossing, then 30 miles back to traverse the same distance. The two governments have been working to remedy the bizarre situation and reopen the border.

THE WORLD: ROUND OR FLAT?

24,901. That's how many miles there are if you circle the earth at the equator. But if you haven't done it, the total might as well be 30,000 miles or 50,000 miles or 100,000 miles. The world might as well be flat.

Say you drive the 561 miles from San Francisco to LA; you only have to do it another 44 times to span the globe. The 210-mile trip from Boston to New York? Only 118 more times. Even if it were possible to drive all the way around the world – a couple of oceans, the Atlantic and the Pacific put the kibosh on this – things might start to seem pretty strange not long after the last Denny's disappeared from your rearview mirror.

Strangeness: that more than anything makes the world seem like an inconceivably big place. The phrase "it might as well be on the other side of the world" denotes anything that seems impossible to imagine or obtain. And although saying "other side" instead of "other end" hints at the world's roundness, let's face it, if places like Kathmandu, Zanzibar or even Paris seem so far as to be impossible to conjure, then the world might as well be flat. Everything unfamiliar is out there

★ 151 ★

someplace, outside of your comfort zone.

But then look what happens when you start traveling: everything starts to shrink. When you've been to the other side of the world, it's obviously no longer impossible to picture. **Begin filling in your passport with stamps, and pretty soon the pieces of the planet start to fall into place.** No longer is it a flat and mysterious expanse. Instead, you see how one place relates to another, and another and another. The entire earth becomes a version of six degrees of separation.

The best way to experience the nearly 25,000-mile circumference of the planet is by flying around the world. You can do it in three flights or dozens, in two days or a year, but once you've gone around, you'll know for sure the earth is round.

❝ Who knew the 24 pages in your passport could hold so much. **❞**

– **CHAD G**, NEW YORK

A Window on the Whole Wide World

On my first trip around the world, I had one flight that went from Singapore to London in daylight. It was as close to being an astronaut as I'll ever be, as a quarter of the globe passed below almost cloud-free. I sat in my window-seat transfixed as the coast of Thailand gave way to the islands of the Indian Ocean, the expanse of India, the desserts and ultra-modern cities of the Arabian Peninsula, the rugged terrain of Eastern Turkey, the iconic snow-capped jaggedness of the Alps and the unmistakable canals of Amsterdam. For your own window on the world, www.airtimetable. com has a good roundup of round-the-world airline tickets. Highly recommended are the plans from the Star Alliance (United Airlines and US Airways) and One World (American Airlines), which let you pay one price and build your own itinerary, choosing from hundreds of cities. For travelers, it's like being a kid in a candy store.

— RYAN VB, CALIFORNIA

BE BOLD

LET'S USE CAPTAIN JAMES T KIRK, THE ORIGINAL *STAR TREK* COMMANDER, AS OUR BOLD-TRAVELER ROLE MODEL. A stay-at-home, pizza-and-beer kind of guy during his early days on Earth, Kirk garnered tremendous self-confidence once he got off the couch and began traveling through the farthest reaches of space. He started small – battling a shape-shifting monster here, smooching an interplanetary babe there. Eventually, though, he came to the point where he could strut around and announce to the galaxy that he'd "boldly go where no man has gone before." A brash statement, but Kirk was pumped full of travelers' confidence.

Using your passport is like enrolling in a cloaked school of in-ternational enterprise. You don't realize you're honing your abilities to be assertive, quick-thinking and self-reliant, as well as sharpening problem-solving and negotiation skills, but the situations you'll find yourself in when you travel abroad strengthen those muscles.

You'll practice assertiveness when you argue with the Turkish carpet seller who has doubled his sales price after pocketing the down payment you left the day prior. When a Chinese money-changer offers you 500 yen for your $85, and the bank exchange rate is 7 to 1, you'll have to think fast to know if it's a good deal. And **self-reliance is a must when it's just you out there, figuring out how to drive a stick-shift rental car through the twisting Alps, or how to find dinner in Jerusalem on Shabbat.** As for negotiating tactics, watch Vietnamese locals go at it beside a bus collision; whoever is the most patient and cool-headed as fists are raised and cigarettes butts are flicked back and forth wins.

Boldness is a sly trait. You may not realize it has taken root until you zip around four lanes of stalled traffic via a highway shoulder (a maneuver picked up from Dakar's Peugeot drivers) or immediately counter a job salary offer (a reflex developed by haggling in India's silk shops).

And that little seed of self-assurance blossoms with each sojourn. Soon you're taking a cue from Kirk and seeking out strange new worlds and new civilizations with your passport: safari touring in Kenya, rock climbing in Thailand, surfing in Australia. Your final frontier keeps moving onward.

"TRAVEL has enriched my life by presenting me with ENDLESS NEW CHALLENGES that foster both INNER STRENGTH AND WISDOM through experiential encounters with the unknown."

– CAROLYN D, CONNECTICUT

THE ART OF BARGAINING

In many countries everything is negotiable, from your hotel rate to that beaded bracelet in the market, even a Coke. These hints should help you find the right price:

Do your homework. Shop around to get a feel for prices. Ask others what they paid for similar products.

Negotiate. Decide on the maximum amount you're willing to pay; start negotiations at half that amount.

Stall. Throw down a pondering "Hmm" or a polite "Is that the best you can do?"

Trade off. If you use cash instead of credit, or buy five items instead of four, can you get a discount? If you promise to pay the higher price, can you get a product upgrade (ie, deluxe room instead of standard, beaded necklace versus beaded bracelet)?

WE'RE DIFFERENT
BUT THE SAME

ACCEPTING HIS NOBEL PEACE PRIZE, THE DALAI LAMA SAID, "When I meet people in different parts of the world, I am always reminded that we are all basically alike: we are all human beings. Maybe we have different clothes, our skin is of a different color, or we speak different languages. That is on the surface. But basically, we are the same human beings. That is what binds us to each other. That is what makes it possible for us to understand each other and to develop friendship and closeness."

Leave it to a Nobel Prize winner, let alone the Dalai Lama, to sum things up perfectly. Having met thousands of people in hundreds of places in dozens of countries, I wholeheartedly agree that we really are all more alike than we are different. And one of the ways we humans are alike is that we are pretty good people. Nothing makes the world seem smaller – and far less scary – than the myriad of random acts of kindness you'll experience on any trip. A few small examples that touched me through the years:

+ Finding myself stranded in the rain late at night in rural France and

DID MY ANCESTORS COME FROM A PLACE JUST LIKE THAT?
>>> REASON No. 17

being picked up by a young Italian couple who wouldn't let me go until I'd found a warm place for the night.

- Having my arm grabbed by an elderly Singaporean man who yanked me off a subway car right before the doors closed and the train trundled off to the yard for the night.

- Stumbling into a wedding party in a remote Vietnamese village and being made the guest of honor.

As you meet more of the people of our planet, it's impossible not to see how much more binds us than separates us. Rich or poor, urban or rural, people want a better world for their children, are protective of those they love and have a basic desire to simply do what's good. Once you've met the locals in whatever place is being called "evil" by so-called leaders who encourage xenophobia in order to achieve their ends, you'll find that not only do you have a lot in common with those in other countries, but their politicians might be saying the same fear-mongering things about you.

> "We talked about how we weren't paid enough in our jobs, how much we liked our friends and whether *Titanic* was really all that good."
>
> – **ROB B**, *after a trip to India*

✳ ✳ ✳

From Big Al to Air Jordan

On my first big trip abroad in 1984, every time I told somebody I was from Chicago, they would do a bad Al Capone impression and make like a machine gun: "Ratta tatta tatta!" This happened from Marrakesh to Oslo. But 10 years later times had changed. This time when I said I was from Chicago, they would break into a big smile and go: "Chicago! Michael Jordan!" From Cambodia to Croatia, I was treated with honor and as a probable close friend of number 23. Thanks, Mike!

– **RYAN VB**, CALIFORNIA

|||||| FROM THE OUTSIDE, WE SURE DO LOOK DIFFERENT. >>> REASON No. **39** ||||||||||||||

FREE YOUR MIND

EVERY PART OF TRAVELING IS A SENSORY-RICH EXPE-RIENCE. Eating the region's spicy specialties, hearing people chat on the street in another mother tongue, discovering the crazy-quilt layout of a town, perusing the unusual headlines in newspapers and thousands of other common-places suddenly become uncommon when you wander around another country.

From disparate elements, a rich portrait emerges – one that's far more complex than any portrayals of a place you encounter in newspapers, on TV or online. One of the great powers of travel is that it removes your blinders. By seeing a place with your own eyes, you discover what's it really about, and doubtless leave wiser than the day you arrived.

Travel shatters so many of our preconceived ideas. Visit Italy, and you may suddenly place a higher value on a lingering meal among friends and return home with a vastly different take on the life-versus-work debate. Or you can journey to India and find yourself confronted with striking ideas about spirituality. The land that gave birth to Buddhism is home to a multiplicity of faiths; that, coupled with the priority Indians place on spiritual affairs, is liable to expand

|||||||||||||| WHO IS THIS BUDDHA YOU KEEP TALKING ABOUT? >>> REASON No. **19** ||||||||||

> "I love being out of my element – discovering that my ways are strange in someone else's eyes."
>
> **– MICHAELA K,** CALIFORNIA

your ideas about how religion fits into daily life.

Even something as innocuous as walking through a market abroad can be a mind-boggling event, as the colors, textures and smells transport you to another realm. When you embark on your trip with openness, even mundane experiences can be deeply enriching. All you need to begin your path to enlightenment is your passport.

Impressions of another country last much longer than the time you were away. **Once you come into contact with another culture, you'll feel like you have a stake in it. Because it's somewhere you've walked, breathed and tasted, and whether your sojourn lasted five days or 50, that place is now somehow a part of you.** That's yet another of the lasting effects of travel: heightening your empathy for a culture and placing its interests among the things that really mean something to you in the world.

Travel: there's nothing else in the world that you can so easily do, and yet receive such immense rewards.

Deep in the Amazon, the Yanomami tribe has lived in communion with the rain forest for centuries. Whereas Westerners view the jungle as an inhospitable place full of poisonous plants and predatory animals, the Yanomami see food, shelter and even clothing and jewelry among the vines and trees. They also see nature's finest pharmacy. The physician's job is the domain of the shaman, who utilizes hundreds

SHAMANS OF THE JUNGLE

of different plants to heal everything from earache to malaria. Originally derided by the scientific community, the shamans' vast knowledge is slowly being recognized and valued in the West. Several drugs have been developed from Amazonian plants, and some believe that cures for AIDS, cancer and other diseases lie hidden in the rain forest. To learn more about it, read *Tales of a Shaman's Apprentice* by Mark J Plotkin.

– REGIS S, INDIANA

||||||||||||||| EVERYONE USED TO SAY THE WORLD WAS FLAT. >>> REASON No. **44** |||||||

TOMORROW STARTS TODAY

★★★

WRITE YOUR OWN LIFE STORY

EVERY TIME I RENEW MY PASSPORT, I MAKE DARN SURE I GET MY OLD ONE BACK. Nowhere can be found a more succinct record of some of my wildest adventures, greatest romances, loneliest moments and more. Think about it: a record of your life that fits in your pocket.

In my first passport (issued July 30, 1984), the very first stamp was Gatwick Airport, near London, at the start of a seven-month trip with a woman who was the love of my life. In the pages that follow are stamps from Hungary, Morocco, Sweden and many more places, all stops on an odyssey for two Americans abroad for the first time. The one from Yugoslavia reminds me of the cold nights we spent in Sarajevo, which seemed filled already with foreboding and a sense of doom, although it would be years before this beautiful town was devastated by civil war. The stamp from Spain reminds me of the wild times we had crashing with some high-living Brits in a beach house until the cops stopped us and said they were about to bust our drug-dealing hosts. We fled.

An elaborate visa with whorls of writing in fountain-pen ink tells of my trip to Afghanistan in 1987. A much more simple stamp from Bangkok's airport in 1989 signaled my first step toward crossing the

> "A ticket is just a piece of paper
> without your passport."
>
> – **JANICE C**, MICHIGAN

border into Cambodia. On both trips I saw far too many examples of man's inhumanity to man (and women and children) and was forever shaken out of my smug complacency. **It's a lot harder to dismiss heart-breaking images on TV when you've seen them for yourself.** Your own passport will record your widening view of the world and your own changing perspective.

All three of my passports are windows into my past, and unlike snapshots, they create vivid images in my head embellished by my own memories. The empty pages of my current passport hold much promise for journeys yet to come. Your passport can do the same for you: it's both a journal of your past and a blank slate of your future.

My Birthday on Bali

On November 2, 1993, I faced an immigration officer at the airport on Bali. I was there on my honeymoon and it was my first visit to a place that over the years I have come to love deeply. But at that moment I was jet-lagged and just a bit giddy. Glancing quickly at my passport, this man noted my birth date (November 8), stamped the page and in a gentle and melodic voice said, "Have a wonderful birthday on Bali." I melted.

– RYAN VB, CALIFORNIA

ONE TRIP IS NEVER ENOUGH

CURBING YOUR SWEET TOOTH AFTER JUST ONE COOKIE IS HARD, but reining in a case of wanderlust is a monumental challenge. Every trip creates yet another craving to see, do and know more. The pursuit of foreign countries and cultures is infectious and lures you farther and farther afield. You may innocently embark on a trip to France and then find that Italy isn't that far away. And, well, gosh, you've never been to Rome, so off you go across the border. Soon you find yourself at the Adriatic. And well, look at that: it's Greece, and since you're on this side of the world, why not? Rarely are trips finite packages.

Invariably, you'll end each trip saying "next time," a hopeful expression of every traveler's wish to depart again for foreign lands to resume the pursuit. Next time you'll start with Greece and follow the scent of ancient empires into Asia Minor. "Why there?" your coworkers might ask. If you answer, "Because it's there," you'll know you're a goner, plain and simple. You've moved beyond travel neophyte to travel junkie, always planning the next trip, the next continent, the next conquest. Here is fine, but there is better.

Traveling abroad certainly is an addiction, but a benign one that challenges your wallet more than your liver. Unlike other obsessions, it's a pursuit of knowledge and experience rather than mere pleasure. It requires full engagement, despite the common misconception that the vagabond life equals escapism.

The habit-forming euphoria comes with everyday successes: finding such basics as food and lodging in a place where no one speaks English. Or careening aboard a rickety fishing boat over white-caps toward a jungle-filled island. **The mother of all highs is when you are the lucky recipient of human kindness – invited to share an afternoon picnic or given a ride when you're lost or stuck.**

Best of all, there's no nasty self-loathing at the end of a trip, unlike a hangover or the sick-to-your-stomach feeling that comes over you after stripping an ice cream carton bare. On the flight home, the after-glow sets in, casting a satisfied half-smile across your face as you sift through memories of strange and wonderful things. Now you know why people treat their passports like treasured lovers.

> **"** Every time I travel abroad, my life is so much richer and I come home with the anticipation of the next place I'm going to visit. **"**
>
> **– MITSIE O,** CALIFORNIA

|||||||||||||||||||||||| ONE BORDER LEADS TO ANOTHER. >>> REASON No. **43** ||||||||||||||||||||

Guardian Angels on the Road

At some point during a trip, the prognosis looks dire. You got on the wrong bus; all the hotels are full; no one understands English. Just as panic starts to darken a tough situation, someone always comes to the rescue. These real-life guardian angels are just ordinary citizens who take the time out of their busy lives to help the confused foreigner on the corner. They offer a ride, advice, hospitality, translations and most of all kindness, making all the obstacles of international travel simply melt away. Then they return back into the fabric of everyday life, like some divine gift of charity. For more stories of real-life angels, read Lonely Planet's *The Kindness of Strangers*.

SHARE THE WEALTH

ALL THE WORLD'S TOURISM RECEIPTS PUT TOGETHER RIVAL THE US ECONOMY in terms of the size of a piggy bank required to house them. Travel is going to take home the gold some day, so there's great opportunity for your around-the-world trip's budget to do heaps of good in countries where many people struggle to earn even the equivalent of $30 a month.

Just going on vacation to a developing country, however, does not mean you're really sharing your wealth. Many travel services – particularly those geared toward package tours – are in fact run by businesses back home. About one in five dollars spent in the Caribbean actually stays in the islands, and only twice as much in Thailand.

Be wary of prepaying for your whole trip at once. Do-it-yourself, pay-to-the-source trips help ensure that more money makes it into locals' hands. Instead of an impersonal hotel, you can opt for a night in a family-run *hospedaje* in Latin America, a mountain village mud hut in Lesotho or an inn booked through a private accommodation service in Europe. It will save you some bucks and give you a look at local life from the inside out. One lady letting rooms in Rome, for example, wouldn't let us leave with wet hair!

Try dining at local restaurants, rather than chains like those you see back home. Noodles made before your eyes in Southeast Asia and slurped on plastic, streetside stools are tasty and cheap. In a neighborhood Czech eatery, they'll assume you'll be having a mug of pilsner before ordering – just like all the locals do.

Instead of buying crafts in fancy hotel shops, go directly to the artisans, who chip away at wood blocks in local shops that sell their traditional masks or chess sets. Rather than quenching your thirst with a Coke, go for a local pop, like Peru's Inca Cola.

Be aware, though, that visiting hill tribes in Southeast Asia or traditional villages in Africa or South America is a particularly sensitive aspect of travel abroad. Do research before signing up for any trip, and question your prospective guide to ensure that local communities are benefiting from tours – and that, in fact, they want you there!

Spending smart is an investment in your own trip. It can also enrich the world.

> **"TRAVEL** is a gift that never disappoints – there's always an **UNEXPECTED ADVENTURE, A FANTASTIC NEW FRIEND, A STARTLING SUNSET** or a **SACRED VIEW."**
>
> – AMY L, NEW YORK

KNOW HOW TO GIVE

A common mistake when visiting developing countries is to routinely hand out gifts – pens, candies, money – to children. It encourages begging, something many locals shake their heads at. It's more respectful to give school supplies to a local school, or toys to a parent. I always bring small gifts from back home – postcards, T-shirts, caps – to have handy when I make a new friend on a bus trip or if I get invited to someone's home.

Because travelers are often able to see more of a country, or region, than locals do (particularly in poorer countries), offering new tourism ideas may help ignite grassroots enterprises. In Vidin, Bulgaria, I suggested that a pal take visitors in his fishing boat to nearby islands he bragged about. Who wouldn't want to frolic on the beach like Bulgarians do?

– ROBERT R, VIRGINIA

I DON'T HAVE A LOT OF DOUGH, BUT I'VE GOT OODLES OF TIME. >>>
REASON No. 51

51

SAVE THE WORLD
(AND YOURSELF)

EVERYBODY WANTS TO CHANGE THE WORLD. But you don't have to be Wonder Woman or Superman to do it. It's something you can even do in your spare time. All you need is some goodwill, a little philanthropic spirit and that little blue book, your passport.

Doing good runs deep in America's bloodstream. And sure, charity starts at home. But why stop there? You'll find your fellow Americans helping out and pitching in at almost any latitude and longitude on the globe. They work for peace and freedom. They provide humanitarian aid to developing nations and rebuild communities after natural disasters. They try to save endangered wildlife and fix up the environment.

What this army of American do-gooders all have in common is their US passport. With one of your own, you can save the world and yourself. Even if it's for only a few days of your vacation, volunteering abroad will exercise your Protestant work ethic, ease your Catholic sense of guilt and improve your cosmic karma. If you're more of a

BUT I'M A SELFISH BASTARD.>>> REASON No. **11**

secular humanist, visualize saving the world's treasures, like the threatened temples at Angkor, Cambodia. Did you know you could even walk the Great Wall of China for charity?

Volunteering is the hands-on way to travel. In just two weeks or less, volunteers can find their way deeper into the soul of a country and experience much more than tourists ever do. **Imagine: instead of slapping a "Free Tibet" sticker on your bumper, with your passport you head to Dharamsala in northern India to help teach English to Tibetan refugees.** Or head to Kenya to help with AIDS education and awareness. It sure beats writing a check.

Volunteering abroad will transform your life even as you improve the lives of others. You connect with strangers who become lifelong friends. Learn a language and other valuable skills, such as teaching or organic farming. You might even build your resume (think of it as "an internship with a view") along the way. Best of all, you'll give someone else a lift along the road to life, liberty and their own pursuit of happiness.

And what you'll get back in return is often so much more than you'll give.

> "Travel is good for the soul and cleans the mind. I swear I am a better person after my travels abroad."
>
> – LAURA B, NEW YORK

Ask Not What Your Country Can Do for You....

At the start of the riotous '60s, Senator John F Kennedy stood on the steps of the University of Michigan's student union. In the middle of the night, he issued a challenge to young Americans: serve your country and work for peace by volunteering to live abroad in Asia, Africa and Latin America. More than 5000 people asked to join the Peace Corps the next year. On August 30, 1961, the program's first volunteers landed in Ghana, where they formed a chorus on the airport tarmac and sang Ghana's national anthem in the local language, Twi. Since that time more than 175,000 Americans have served as Peace Corps volunteers in almost 140 countries. For more inspiring, touching and funny stories from everyday people who had their lives changed by joining the Peace Corps, surf to **www.peacecorps.gov** and click on "What's It Like to Volunteer?".

★ 175 ★

LIFE
MAY NEVER BE THE SAME

IT'S NOT YET DAYBREAK AS TWO TRAVELERS FOLLOW A WINDING PATH INTO THE RAIN FOREST. Enormous temples rise up all around them. Even in the dark, they can see the elaborate stonework of this civilization that mysteriously disappeared. The two climb to the top of one of the pyramids, where they can see far out over the jungle canopy. An indigo sky, growing lighter by the minute, forms the backdrop for brightly plumed birds flitting from tree to tree, the sounds of monkeys chattering and all the other animals of the rain forest slowly coming to life as the sun rises over the ancient Mayan city of Tikal, Guatemala.

This is just the beginning. Perhaps it's a love story, an adventure tale or the moment of epiphany in a bildungsroman. Like the trip that awaits you, too, their future is wide open. And now the story shifts as we introduce an even more important character, namely you.

Regardless of where or when you travel, you're unlikely to return unchanged. With your passport, traveling abroad brings dramatic new perspectives, deeper understanding of cultures and a kind of wisdom about the world.

Once you've walked the streets of another country, shared a meal with local villagers and experienced a foreign way of life in all its rawness and beauty, that place becomes a part of you. Seeing the museums and markets and hearing the music are all a rich part of the travel experience, but it's the people you meet who will leave a deep and lasting impression. **This is why travel is one of the greatest tools for promoting peace; after you've spent time with another country's citizens, you can't imagine waging war on them.**

Travel can bring enormous changes in your life. You may meet your life partner while traveling. You may decide to live abroad or pursue a new job upon your return. Travel may open the door to a newfound spirituality or ignite a long-dormant passion for photography, painting, music or writing. One of the great joys of traveling is opening yourself up to the unexpected. The only question is, Are you ready to take the journey?

★ 177 ★

AN UNEXPECTED PATH.

When I set out on my first big trip to Latin America, I had only nebulous goals in mind. I would start in Mexico City and head south, learning Spanish along the way. I saved enough money to travel for six months, gave up my apartment and took off. I was young, full of wanderlust and incredibly naive. Although the trip turned out differently than I expected, it awakened my passion for traveling and filled me with dreams. Upon my return, I gave up advertising and started writing articles. One thing led to another, and my travel-writing career took off. It all began with a trip into the unknown, and led to discovering one of my life's greatest joys. — **REGIS S**, INDIANA

"Traveling made me realize how little I really needed in the world. In India I was living out of a backpack and surrounded by people pursuing simple, compassionate lives, and I've never been happier." — NANCY S, MICHIGAN

★ 178 ★

APPENDIX

Browse Lonely Planet's comprehensive catalog of guidebooks, maps, travel references and illustrated books at www.lonelyplanet.com. Also visit www.lonelyplanet.com/passport for more passport information. The following resources can also help jump-start your journey abroad.

Useful Travel Organizations

ACCESSIBLE JOURNEYS (☎800-846-4537; www.disabilitytravel.com)
Wheelchair-accessible group tours of Canada, Europe, the Middle East, Africa and Asia starting at $1950 (excluding airfare).

ACTION WITHOUT BORDERS (☎212-843-3973; www.idealist.org)
A free online database of jobs, internships and volunteer opportunities in more than 160 countries.

ALLIANCE ABROAD (☎866-622-7623; www.allianceabroad.com)
Study, work, volunteer and language-immersion programs in Europe, Latin America, Australia and Asia. Program fees vary.

ALYSON ADVENTURES (☎800-825-9766; www.alysonadventures.com)
Award-winning gay adventure travel vacations in Australia, New Zealand, the Caribbean, Europe and Asia.

ARTIS (☎800-232-6893; www.artis-tours.org)
Nonprofit art study tours of France, Italy, Greece, China and Indonesia. One month in Italy (including classes, flight and accommodation) costs $4195.

ARTISANS OF LEISURE (☎800-214-8144; www.artisansofleisure.com)
Luxury tours around the globe, for example, a nine-day culinary tour of Thailand ($3745) or a 12-day trip that zips from Paris to Morocco and back ($8590). Tour prices exclude airfare to/from the start/end point.

AUDUBON SOCIETY (☎800-967-7425; www.audubon.org)
Natural history programs focusing on conservation, education and enjoyment. One-week international trips start at $2150 (excluding airfare).

BACKROADS (☎800-462-2848; www.backroads.com)
Active and adventure travel tours of Canada, Europe, Latin America and Asia. Specialty trips available for families, solo travelers and students, as well as multisport fanatics.

CIEE: COUNCIL ON INTERNATIONAL EDUCATIONAL EXCHANGE
(☎ 800-407-8839; www.ciee.org)
Study, volunteer and work abroad opportunities worldwide from long-standing US-based organization.

CLASSIC JOURNEYS (☎ 800-200-3887; www.classicjourneys.com)
Cultural walking adventures, culinary tours and family journeys in Canada, Europe, Latin America, Africa and the Asia-Pacific region. With an average group size of just 10 people, tours are led by full-time local guides.

COUNTRY WALKERS (☎ 800-464-9255; www.countrywalkers.com)
Walking tours in destinations around the world, from Canada to Bhutan. Special trips available for families or foodies.

CROSS-CULTURAL SOLUTIONS (☎ 800-380-4777; www.crossculturalsolutions.org)
Volunteer programs in Latin and South America, Asia, Africa and Russia. Professional in-country support included in the program fee. One-week trips start at $1400 (excluding airfare).

CUISINE INTERNATIONAL (☎ 214-373-1161; www.cuisineinternational.com)
Award-winning weeklong cooking schools in Italy, France, England, Portugal and Brazil.

EARTHWATCH INSTITUTE (☎ 800-776-0188; www.earthwatch.org)
Short-term volunteer opportunities assisting scientists with field research, usually requiring no special qualifications. The cost of participating in a one- to three-week expedition ranges from $1600 to $4000 (excluding airfare).

ELDERHOSTEL (☎ 877-426-8056; www.elderhostel.org)
Popular, nonprofit educational programs abroad for those aged 55 or older, with international trips everywhere from Argentina to Zambia. Some programs include outdoor activities, home stays or journeys by rail or ship.

EF TOURS (☎ 800-637-8222; www.eftours.com)
Programs designed to help travelers become guides leading education-based tours around the world.

GLOBAL CROSSROAD (☎ 800-413-2008; www.globalcrossroad.com)
Volunteer and internship programs in Latin and South America, Asia and Africa. Two-week volunteer vacations start at $1000 (excluding airfare). Special summer cultural and educational programs for 18- to 27-year-olds include home stays and a week of sightseeing.

GLOBAL VOLUNTEERS (☎ 800-487-1074; www.globalvolunteers.org)
Many short-term volunteer opportunities in community development programs worldwide. For example, spending two weeks helping orphaned kids in Peru costs $2100, including room and board (but not airfare).

GLOBE AWARE (☎ 877-588-4562; www.globeaware.org)
Volunteer placements for individuals and groups in programs often coordinated by a local community leader. Trips to Latin and South America, Asia and the Caribbean (including Cuba) start at $1050 (excluding airfare).

HEIFER INTERNATIONAL (☎ 800-422-0474; www.heifer.org)
"Educational travel with a purpose" by a nonprofit organization dedicated to ending poverty and world hunger. Study tours to Europe, Latin America, the Caribbean, Africa, Asia or South Pacific start at $2000 (excluding airfare).

I-TO-I (☎ 800-985-4864; www.i-to-i.com)
Volunteer opportunities in education, conservation, community development, media, sports, health, marketing and tourism projects on all continents. Two-week trips cost $1200 and up (excluding airfare).

LANGUAGES ABROAD (☎ 800-219-9924; www.languagesabroad.com)
Liaison between international-language schools and those who wish to study a language abroad. A one-week program in Oaxaca, Mexico, costs $450 (excluding airfare) for 20 small-group Spanish lessons, room and board with a host family and daily cultural exchange activities.

MOBILITY INTERNATIONAL USA (☎ 541-343-1284; www.miusa.org)
Cross-cultural experiences for people with disabilities around the world. Exchange programs may include home stays, cultural learning or outdoor activities. A two-week cross-cultural leadership exchange trip to Japan for young adults starts at $850 (including airfare).

MOUNTAIN TRAVEL SOBEK (☎ 888-687-6235; www.mtsobek.com)
Hundreds of adventure tours abroad, such as climbing in the Alps, trekking in the Himalayas or sea-kayaking in the Galapagos Islands. Ten-day trips start at $2500 (excluding airfare).

OUTWARD BOUND WILDERNESS (www.outwardboundwilderness.org)
Small-group youth expeditions to the Caribbean, South America or Europe. Students can earn academic credit, learn survival skills and clean up the environment on 10-day international courses, starting at $2500 (excluding airfare).

PEACE CORPS (☎ 800-424-8580; www.peacecorps.gov)
Volunteer opportunites in more than 70 countries around the world. Live-abroad projects focus on education, youth outreach and community development, business development, the environment, agriculture, information technology, or health and HIV/AIDS.

REI ADVENTURES (☎ 800-622-2236; www.rei.com/adventures)
International adventure trips focusing on outdoor activities, from heli-hiking to active birding. Specialty trips available for families or women travelers.

SIERRA CLUB (☎ 415-977-5500; www.sierraclub.org)
Outdoor activity, activist and volunteer service trips around the globe. Two-week international trips start at $2000 (excluding airfare).

UNITED NATIONS VOLUNTEERS (www.unvolunteers.org)
Volunteer opportunities for skilled professionals with five years of work experience. Foreign language skills desirable. Successful applicants receive a volunteer living allowance during their assignments.

US DEPARTMENT OF STATE CONSULAR SECTION
(☎ 877-487-2778, TDD/TTY 888-874-7793; http://travel.state.gov)
Information on how to renew, replace or apply for a passport. Also, details on visa requirements, health conditions, minor political disturbances, unusual currency regulations and crime and security information for every country in the world. Check for recent public announcements and travel warnings when planning trips.

VOLUNTEERS FOR PEACE (☎ 802-259-2759; www.vfp.org)
Nearly 3000 short-term international work-camp programs in more than 90 countries. Participants live and work with other volunteers from all over the world. Fees are reasonable, starting at $250 for two or three weeks.

WILDERNESS VENTURES (☎ 800-533-2281; www.wildernessventures.com)
Summer adventure travel programs for young adults in Europe, Australia and the Caribbean. Three-week trips cost $4000 and up (excluding airfare).

WORKINGABROAD (www.workingabroad.com)
Unusual volunteer opportunities (eg, in cultural development, environmental restoration, indigenous rights or traditional art and music), available via an online network. Website offers trip reports from the field.

52 ESSENTIAL TRAVEL WEBSITES

Click to the "Travel Links" section of the Lonely Planet website (www.lonelyplanet.com) to find hundreds of travel websites.

TRAVEL AGENTS & DISCOUNTS
www.11thhourvacations.com
www.counciltravel.com
www.expedia.com
www.hotels.com
www.orbitz.com
www.priceline.com
www.qixo.com
www.sidestep.com
www.site59.com
www.skyauction.com
www.smartertravel.com
www.statravel.com
www.travelocity.com
www.travelzoo.com

SPECIAL TRAVEL INTERESTS
www.access-able.com
www.adventuredivas.com
www.adventuretraveltips.com
www.backdoorjobs.com
www.thebathroomdiaries.com
www.bootsnall.com
www.coffeeshopdirect.com
www.couchsurfing.com
www.escapeartist.com
www.familytravelboards.com
www.thefamilytravelfiles.com

www.festivals.com
www.gonomad.com
www.guinnessworldrecords.com
www.journeywoman.com
http://language.schoolexplorer.com
www.mindmyhouse.com
www.purpleroofs.com
www.rosettaproject.org
www.slowfood.com
www.southernseaventures.com
www.spafinder.com
www.transitionsabroad.com
www.travelfilms.org
www.travelwithyourkids.com

OTHER TRAVEL INFORMATION
www.airtimetable.com
www.cia.gov/cia/publications/factbook
www.cdc.gov/travel
www.customs.ustreas.gov/xp/cgov/travel
www.independenttraveler.com
www.johnnyjet.com
www.mdtravelhealth.com
www.seatguru.com
www.trainweb.com
www.tripadvisor.com
www.weather.com
www.who.int/ith
http://world.altavista.com

Behind the Scenes

This book is the result of lots of hard work by lots of dedicated passport-toting people. The initial project team comprised Laetitia Clapton, Robin Goldberg, Don George, Cindy Cohen, Aimée Goggins, Mindi Ehrlich, Gary Todoroff, Candice Jacobus, Janet Swainson and Todd Sotkiewicz. The book was commissioned out of Lonely Planet's London and Oakland offices by Laetitia Clapton and Sara "Sam" Benson, who was also the coordinating author. Candice Jacobus art-directed the project with Julia Flagg from Flagg Design designing the internals and laying out the book and Daniel New designing the cover. Erin Corrigan managed production of the book, which was edited by Valerie Sinzdak and proofed by Erin. Jo Vraca and Graham Imeson coordinated print production. Julie Deaton managed the marketing and her team included Candice Jacobus, Aimee Goggins, Jesse Fankushen, Cindy Cohen, Frank Ruiz, Robin Goldberg, Mindi Ehrlich, Jenn Roberts and Greg Mand. Many people, including the entire Oakland office, helped us in the making of this book. As well as a huge thanks to the people credited above, thanks go to: Jane Pennells, Roz Hopkins, Tamara Barr, Kathleen Munnelly, Jain Lemos, David Zingarelli, Angie Ryan, Mary Hollowell, Brice Gosnell, Jennye Garibaldi, Michaela Klink, Amy Luning, Karen Finlay, Michael Kohn, Neil Wilson, Quentin Frayne, Matt Phillips, Rik Mulder, Karin Vidstrup Monk, Jeremy Goldberg and an anonymous Norwegian lady in a café. And finally, thanks of course to Phil Keoghan, Tony Wheeler and our wonderful authors whose infectious enthusiasm for travel leaps out of every page.

From the Authors

Sara "Sam" Benson Thanks to Laetitia Clapton, Candice Jacobus, Robin Goldberg, Julie Deaton and the rest of the crackerjack Passports team, especially Don George for thinking of me. All of my co-authors generously gave of their time and talents, notably Karla Z, Thomas K and Robert R. Big thanks to Josh for checking everything twice and to my parents for getting their passports, just in case. Dōmo arigatō gozaimashita to the Imai family of Hiroshima, Japan, and Mazda Motor Corporation for sponsoring my first trip overseas.

Chris Baty Thanks to Sam for the kind-hearted invitation to participate in the project. Thanks as well to my highly professional team of romantic translators: Paul Burgin, Wendy Smith, Michele Posner and that random Norwegian woman from the coffee shop. And a huge "You're the Best!" stamp to my parents for encouraging an impressionable fifteen-year-old version of myself to go study in France that fateful summer.

Tom Downs Thanks to Laetitia and Sam for pulling me into this unique project. Thanks to American Airlines for handing me that first free flight to Paris. Heart-filled gratitude to Fawnzie.

Julie Grundvig A big thanks goes to Yipeng and Mulan for standing by me through all sorts of crazy adventures – the time you got me off of that sinking ship will not be forgotten! Thanks to Sam Benson and Laetitia Clapton for involving me with this project. And a special thanks to my grandmother for inspiring me to leave the country in the first place.

Thomas Kohnstamm Thanks first to Sam and Laetitia for involving me in this book and again to Sam for her support throughout the writing process. My personal travel story never would have gotten off the ground without my parents. Thanks to them for taking me on my first (overly ambitious, as usual) trip abroad from England to Egypt to the Eastern Bloc and back – by car. Also thanks to the town of Jaca, Spain, where I got my first taste of solo travel.

Robert Reid Thanks go to Mai for putting up with this lifestyle; Sam Benson and Laetitia Clapton for offering the fun deal and being great to work with; and the Pyramid of the Sun at Teotíhuacan outside Mexico City where, at age 5, it all started.

Regis St Louis Big thanks to Laetitia Clapton and Sam Benson for inviting me on board the passport ship. *Beijos* to Cassandra for supporting my nomadic lifestyle. Thanks also go to my parents for taking me to Yugoslavia and later encouraging me to study something totally impractical (Slavic languages anyone?), which nonetheless brought me to magical places I never even dreamed of going.

Ryan Ver Berkmoes I owe my parents a huge debt (literally!) for getting me out on the road early. Later on the first big trip to Europe, my mother Lucille found ways to wire us money in weird places that saved our bacon while buying same in that non-ATM era. I also owe a huge debt to the many friends and relatives whose companionship immeasurably added to my joy of travel and to those I met along the way who did likewise. No trip is complete without a welcome home from Erin Corrigan, and they are far better when she's along for the ride.

China Williams Thanks to my hubby, Matt, for chauffering me to the airport on various sojourns. Sam Benson and Laetitia Clapton for wanting to print my blathering. And to Herr Lader and the town of Forsheim, Germany, for putting up with me on my maiden journey.

Karla Zimmerman Thanks to mom and dad for hauling me through most of the Lower 48, and later backing my first international trip to Madrid and beyond (I'd still be playing harmonica in Athens' airport earning change to get home, if not for you). Thanks to Sam for encouragement and patience. Über-thanks to Eric, the ultimate traveling companion who smiles throughout all the insanity.